No Matter What

DEALING WITH ADVERSITY IN SOBRIETY

Stories from AA Grapevine

T0163771

BOOKS PUBLISHED BY AA GRAPEVINE, INC.

The Language of the Heart (& eBook)
The Best of the Grapevine Volumes I, II, III
The Best of Bill (& eBook)
Thank You for Sharing
Spiritual Awakenings (& eBook)
I Am Responsible: The Hand of AA
The Home Group: Heartbeat of AA (& eBook)
Emotional Sobriety — The Next Frontier (& eBook)
Spiritual Awakenings II (& eBook)
In Our Own Words: Stories of Young AAs in Recovery (& eBook)
Beginners' Book (& eBook)
Voices of Long-Term Sobriety (& eBook)
A Rabbit Walks Into A Bar
Step by Step — Real AAs, Real Recovery (& eBook)
Emotional Sobriety II — The Next Frontier (& eBook)
Young & Sober (& eBook)
Into Action (& eBook)
Happy, Joyous & Free (& eBook)
One on One (& eBook)
No Matter What (& eBook)
Grapevine Daily Quote Book (& eBook)
Sober & Out (& eBook)
Forming True Partnerships (& eBook)
Our Twelve Traditions (& eBook)
Making Amends (& eBook)
Voices of Women in AA (& eBook)
AA in the Military (& eBook)
One Big Tent (& eBook)
Take me to your Sponsor (& eBook)

IN SPANISH
El lenguaje del corazón
Lo mejor de Bill (& eBook)
El grupo base: Corazón de AA
Lo mejor de La Viña
Felices, alegres y libres (& eBook)
Un día a la vez (& eBook)
Frente A Frente (& eBook)
Bajo El Mismo Techo (& eBook)

IN FRENCH
Le langage du coeur
Les meilleurs articles de Bill
Le Groupe d'attache: Le battement du coeur des AA
En tête à tête (& eBook)
Heureux, joyeux et libres (& eBook)
La sobriété émotive

No Matter What

DEALING WITH ADVERSITY IN SOBRIETY

Stories from AA Grapevine

AAGRAPEVINE,Inc.
New York, New York
WWW.AAGRAPEVINE.ORG

ISBN: 978-1-938413-25-4

Fourth Printing 2024

AA PREAMBLE

Alcoholics Anonymous is a fellowship of people
who share their experience, strength and hope
with each other that they may solve their common problem
and help others to recover from alcoholism.

The only requirement for membership is a desire to stop drinking.
There are no dues or fees for AA membership; we are self-
supporting through our own contributions. AA is not allied with
any sect, denomination, politics, organization or institution;
does not wish to engage in any controversy, neither endorses nor
opposes any causes.

Our primary purpose is to stay sober
and help other alcoholics to achieve sobriety.

©AA Grapevine, Inc.

CONTENTS

AA Preamble v

Welcome xi

PART ONE: PHYSICAL ADVERSITY

CHAPTER ONE: Accepting the Unacceptable

AAs share how they cope with persistent pain or lingering illness

Stumbling Block to Stepping-Stone *February 2007* 2

No Reason to Drink *February 1995* 4

The Littlest Things *May 1997* 4

Loving Arms *November 2004* 6

The Courage of Friends *May 2005* 7

Only Love Has Meaning *June 1989* 10

At My Age *March 2009* 14

CHAPTER TWO: My Greatest Test So Far

Members who are deaf, blind, or otherwise disabled do whatever it takes to get to meetings, stay sober, and carry the message

Speak Up! *September 2010* 18

An Inner Truth *May 2007* 19

Wills and Ways *December 2006* 21

The Hand of AA *February 2000* 22

No Need to Be Alone *October 1990* 25

An Important Secret *July 2001* 26

Blindsided *April 2010* 27

PART TWO: EMOTIONAL ADVERSITY

CHAPTER THREE: Life Will Keep on Happening

Seeking help for their fear, anxiety, depression, or mental illness helped these alcoholics move forward in recovery

Unreasonable Fears *July 2010* 30

Many Do Recover *April 2004* 31

Living Life Forward *October 2005* 31

Life—It Happens *May 2005* 33

A New Perspective *February 2006* 35

Falling Apart on the Inside *April 2005* 36

An Outside Issue? *October 2005* 39

CHAPTER FOUR: Not in My Life Boat: When Love and Tolerance Fail Us

Letting go of resentments and judgments about fellow AAs

The Watering Hole *September 2003* 42

Shake My Hand *December 2010* 44

Memoirs of a Black AA *August 1985* 45

Sinking Fast *May 2010* 47

Another Story *January 2004* 49

A Plea for Love and Tolerance *April 1999* 50

At Home in a Home Group *February 1991* 51

Babies Are Not Us? *March 2010* 52

CHAPTER FIVE: To Love and Be Loved

Members reach out for help—and to help others—when heartache and loneliness threaten to shatter their sobriety

Self-Support *July 2007* 54

Life, Not Regrets *July 2007* 57

Love and Death—One Day at a Time *February 2003*. 58

Riding It Out *July 1997*. 59

Adult Love *January 2004* 63

In the Center of Sorrow *February 2007*. 65

Gruff Love *October 2006*. 68

PART THREE: FINANCIAL ADVERSITY

CHAPTER SIX: Paycheck to Paycheck, Meeting to Meeting

*Unemployed AAs hold on to hope and the Fellowship
one day at a time*

Fired Up! *September 2010* 72

Out of Work, But Not Hope *December 2000*. 73

Through the Darkest Days *May 2005*. 74

Eyeliner, Anyone? *July 2004* 78

The Phone Fix *December 2001*. 80

Dependence on His Higher Power Led Him to
a Greater Sense of Independence *October 1979* 81

Lifetime Dream *March 2010*. 83

CHAPTER SEVEN: Sober, Grateful, Broke

*The big and small coincidences (or maybe miracles) that carry
recovering alcoholics through tough economic times*

Tax Man *December 2009* 86

New Boots *March 2010* 89

No Spares *October 2010* 90

Gimme Shelter *March 2010*. 91

The Trap Door *August 1996*. 93

The Woman in the Mirror *June 1998* 95

PART FOUR: SPIRITUAL ADVERSITY

CHAPTER EIGHT: The End of the Journey

Realizing that their days are soon drawing to a close, these AAs reaffirm their desire to stay sober

Just an Attitude *April 2002*...98
Living Sober, Dying Sober *September 2004* 99
Serenity Garden *September 2010* 101
Grace and Dignity *September 2004*.....................................103
No Excuse to Drink *August 1996*.......................................104
Another Chance *June 2003*..106
Living Sober *April 2001*..107

CHAPTER NINE: Through Many Dark Valleys

Money problems, health problems, relationship problems— AAs have the tools to face any adversity life hands them

Size 8, Extra Wide *January 2001* 110
A Life Without Problems *May 2007*.....................................114
A Great Loss Made Him Even
More Grateful for AA *February 1980* 116
Fire in the Holler *October 1987*.......................................118
How the Universe Works *November 2006* 120
A Horse Named Zachary *February 2004* 121
The Care of God *December 1999*..125
Relief Pitcher *February 2007*..127
My Best Day Sober *December 2000* 128

Twelve Steps 130
Twelve Traditions...131
About AA and AA Grapevine..132

Welcome

"We have seen AAs suffer lingering and fatal illness with little complaint, and often in good cheer. ... We have some members who never seem to get on their feet moneywise, and still others who encounter heavy financial reverses. Ordinarily we see these situations met with fortitude and faith."
— Essay on Step Twelve, *Twelve Steps and Twelve Traditions*

All recovering alcoholics have had to deal with adversity at multiple points in sobriety. Defined as a state of hardship or affliction, adversity could be an ugly divorce, the death of a child, the loss of a house to fire (or to the bank), or the discovery that you have a serious illness. Despite the pain we are in when these tragedies strike, drinking is not an option. We cannot drink again, as it would only lead to worse calamity. For those who have gone through the Twelve Steps, perhaps two or more times, the answers should be obvious: We talk to our sponsor or other AAs. We go to more meetings. We turn it over to our Higher Power, however we define he, she, it or they. We help another alcoholic. Does it work?

AA co-founder Bill W., sober for about 17 years by the time he penned *Twelve Steps and Twelve Traditions*, knew all too well the ups and downs of a sober life. In his essay on Step Twelve, he wrote: "How shall we come to terms with seeming failure or success? Can we now accept and adjust to either without despair or pride? Can we accept poverty, sickness, loneliness, and bereavement with courage and serenity? Can we steadfastly content ourselves with the humbler, yet sometimes more durable, satisfactions when the brighter, more glittering achievements are denied us?

"The AA answer to these questions about living is 'Yes, all of these things are possible.' We know this because we see monotony, pain, and even calamity turned to good use by those who keep on trying to practice AA's Twelve Steps," he continued. "Of course all AAs, even the best, fall far short of such achievements as a consistent thing. Without necessarily taking that first drink, we often get quite far off the beam."

As the stories in this collection show, it is not just outside forces that spell adversity. Often the alcoholic's trouble is of his own making—a resentment that won't die, a bout of self-pity over not having a partner, a desire for revenge that the member cannot seem to extinguish. Or it is an untreated emotional difficulty coming to the surface, letting the AA know she must finally swallow her pride and seek help.

Some things are in our power to change; others we have to simply accept. The AAs in the stories that follow have taken both paths. Some situations are very difficult to change, and if it's acceptance that's needed, acceptance might be a long time coming. But through prayer and meditation, making use of a particular Step, or working with others, each member finally reckons with his adversity.

PART ONE
PHYSICAL ADVERSITY

CHAPTER 1
ACCEPTING THE UNACCEPTABLE

AAs share how they cope with persistent pain or lingering illness

Chronic illness and near-constant pain can whittle away the spirit of even the most positive, loving and accepting AA member. Some write about the despair and hopelessness they felt upon learning of their condition. One member, dealing with a painful permanent condition, prayed about it, asking God if this was his idea of a sadistic joke. Another, considering suicide when her condition worsened, raged at her Higher Power, asking if he'd abandoned her. As time moved on, some got a little better and their pain was eased. But others simply took their illness one day at a time, staying close to AA and finding ways to remain useful, active members.

Stumbling Block to
Stepping-Stone FEBRUARY 2007

With a new associate's degree in human services, Army training as a behavioral science specialist, and three years of experience as a counselor, I was ready.

But just as I began sending resumes to prospective employers, I became permanently disabled with a condition that frequently confines me to bed. After about two hours, I must take medication my doctor prescribes or pain forces me back into bed. I can spend about twenty minutes at the computer.

I know the God of my understanding has a sense of humor; I've seen examples all of my life, but didn't recognize it until I got sober. So when I prayed, I said, "If this is your idea of a joke, it's sadistic. (Poor me, poor me.) Father, did you really carry me all this way just to drop me?" It didn't sound like the God of my understanding.

I continued with my "poor me" attitude for a while, hoping that medical treatment would help me get back to work. I spent—or wasted—about six months with this mind-set and let my character defects run the show.

While meditating one afternoon, I remembered some advice given by the late actor Bruce Lee: "Turn the stumbling block into a stepping-stone."

I examined my motives. Had I chosen the human services field for recognition? Was I looking to inflate my ego? Or did I have an honest desire to help those in need? I thought about my time as a counselor in the army. Although I frequently received commendations, I realized that my real reward came the moment I saw the light of hope replace the look of despair in a soldier's eyes.

I prayed and meditated again, asking God for direction. How could I serve his will rather than my own?

That same night, I got a phone call from a longtime acquaintance in the Fellowship. It was three o'clock in the morning, and she was in a hopeless state of despair. I got dressed and drove to her house. We sat at her kitchen table and talked for more than three hours. Now, that's what I call a fast response from my Higher Power!

I suddenly understood that even in bed I could answer my phone. I knew our local AA hotline had trouble getting volunteers. Calls were forwarded from the intergroup office to a member's home phone, or even a cell phone. Because I wasn't working, I was available twenty-four hours a day.

I got a glimpse of God's will for me: I could be a hand of AA. I made it known—especially to newcomers—that I was available twenty-four hours a day. Happily, I reached out to newcomers, sponsees, and even some of those who had been sober for "a few twenty-four hours."

Not only do I feel useful and productive again, I also feel that I am carrying out God's will, which is not too different from my own. Sometimes we get what we ask for, but not always in the way we imagine. The stumbling block of an inability to work became a stepping-stone to doing what I love best—helping those in a state of crisis.

If I have learned anything from this experience, it's to have faith and look for clues to the will of my Higher Power. I also need to keep my ego out of the way and let God drive the bus. I do it one day at a time, one step at a time—even if the stepping-stone at first looks like a stumbling block.

ED S.
Scranton, Pennsylvania

No Reason to Drink FEBRUARY 1995
(From Dear Grapevine)

I've been in AA for nearly two years. In the beginning, I couldn't understand why people were always saying that they were sober "by the grace of God." Now, after going through some rough times, I've learned a lot.

In June of 1994, I got very sick and found out I had full-blown AIDS; I had not known I was HIV positive. I lost weight rapidly, going from 168 to 139 pounds in two weeks. At that point, the Third Step came to me right away. I turned my life and will over to the care of God as I understood him. And you know, things do get better.

Now I have two diseases, one being alcoholism and the other being AIDS. But there is still no reason for me to drink!

LARRY E.
Pahrump, Nevada

The Littlest Things MAY 1997
(Excerpt)

When I poured out my last bottle—what I pray was my last bottle—I again trembled with fear. In my heart, I knew that if my multiple sclerosis (MS) got worse, I'd surely drink myself into the ground. No one would dare to stop me. After all, if my MS got worse, I would deserve to drink.

MS is a chronic, disabling, and incurable neurological disease that steals from its victims many physical abilities most people take for granted. It's particularly cruel in that it steals these things spo-radically, and then if one is lucky, it just as sporadically gives them back, until the next exacerbation. MS has taught me to thank God for things that most people take for granted: the ability to see, to speak, to walk, even the ability to go to the bathroom.

In the summer of 1995, my worst nightmare came true. The symptoms got so bad that I was no longer able to perform my job. Within weeks, I got worse and for the first time in my life, I was actively suicidal. My rage at God soared. Sobbing uncontrollably, I screamed at God, "Why have you abandoned me?"

Initially, I had a burning resentment against anyone with strong legs. My anger served as an iron shield, and I refused to remove it for fear God would send me still more pain.

I didn't want to ask for help. I wanted everyone to marvel at how stoically I coped with adversity; and I hated to bother people. I figured they were too busy doing more important things with far more important people than me. But without a drink, it's tough to be stoic. Once I was able to swallow my pride and pick up that hun-dred-pound telephone, I discovered that there were a few people in AA who actually cared about me. For example, when MS affected my ability to drive to meetings, a friend gave me a lift.

Much to my amazement, I survived that summer from hell and have regained some of the physical abilities I lost. Every morning, I thank God for the ability to see my partner and my cats, to hear the birds outside my window and to hobble over to my meditation chair, where I start the day with a prayer.

Eventually, I realized that God hadn't abandoned me at all but that I'd abandoned him. Yesterday, missing my old body, I burst into tears for the umpteenth time and tasted that old craving for a bottle of wine. Just go to the liquor store and get a bottle, I told myself. It will make everything feel better.

Instead, I picked up the phone and called my sponsor, even though I knew she was at work. Sometimes it's easier for me to talk to an answering machine. Then, because I still wanted to drink, I picked up the phone again and called another friend, who was able to talk on the job.

I've never taken my sobriety for granted because I know I'm only one drink away from ruining my life. Having MS can be hard some days, but doing it sober usually makes it tolerable one day at a time. Each day, I ask God for serenity to accept the unacceptable. The Big Book never promised me a life without problems (although I still keep looking for it between the lines).

If anyone had told me I'd still be sober despite MS, I would have thrown a drink in their face. Learning to live life on life's terms— not on my terms—has been the ultimate miracle. If you're new or coming back, don't quit before your own miracle happens.

MARSHA Z.
Jamaica Plain, Massachusetts

Loving Arms NOVEMBER 2004
(From Dear Grapevine)

In reference to "The Band Played On" (June 2004), I have been HIV+ for almost twenty-five years and have been living with AIDS since 1995. I got sober in AA in 1998. My fear was that being a gay man with HIV, I was doomed to be left out and alone with both my diseases. However, over the past six years, AA has provided every need that has come up for me both in sobriety and in my AIDS situation. I have been close to death over five times in the past six years and literally hundreds of AA members have come to my side bearing unconditional love and acceptance. I have had married men come to stay with me for two to three days at a time and feed me, change my bed clothes, and bathe me when I could barely sit up in bed. I have never wanted nor needed anything that an AA member wasn't willing to supply me. AA also provided the most loving and caring man as a live-in attendant to assist me when I have seizures. One mens' meeting has an "Everett" commitment, which means that I never have to find a ride to a meeting. So I don't fear for the future, because I am in the loving arms of AA.

EVERETT A.
Santa Monica, California

The Courage of Friends MAY 2005

I have been sober for twenty-three years. It is often voiced in AA meetings that God will find you a parking spot, "right in front of the meeting" and that nothing bad can happen to you once you're sober. When I came into AA, I believed this too. Now, I do not think God is at all interested in my daily existence. I believe there is some Higher Power, because I cannot otherwise explain why I haven't had a drink. But God is not some loving power or guiding force in my life. God makes decisions and I live with them. Last July I was diagnosed with colon/rectal cancer. I had been suffering with a chronic illness for some time before this and he wasn't very helpful. I prayed, but God did not cure me of this malady, nor did he send doctors to help me, although God knows I saw enough of them. Nor did he supply me with the kind of courage I needed to face my dilemma. My friends are a different story.

I have wonderful friends in AA, but I had no idea how wonderful. After I found out about the cancer, the first phone call I made was to my friend Vic. Vic had cancer the year before and he immediately invited me to stay with him for my first couple of weeks out of the hospital, knowing I wouldn't be able to take care of myself. This was only the beginning. I had friends call who I had not heard from in years. People I didn't know called every day and others volunteered to do anything I might need. I was quite surprised at the response to my illness. I had always seen myself as a bit of a curmudgeon and thought that people tolerated me more than appreciated me. I was learning otherwise. It is very difficult for me to accept help. It is easy to give help because in some ways that doesn't really involve me. But accepting help in a gracious way from people who are offering it graciously is a much more difficult task. When I began to take the cure—an operation, chemo, and radiation therapy—I was told it would be a six-to-eight-month process. I was not looking forward to the "journey."

At this time, I had a young, healthy girlfriend named Anne-Margaret. We had been together for two years, and it was the best time I had ever had. She was lovely and full of life and wanted to do everything. Her mother called it flying around. "Anne-Margaret's out flying around," she would say. Anne-Margaret kept me from taking myself too seriously and, along with my AA friends, made my life bearable—almost enjoyable.

When I was ready to go home, my sister came to look after me for a week. People from AA called and left messages and sent emails every day to find out if I was all right and if there was something they could do. They brought over sandwiches, books, magazines, and videotapes. When they found out I didn't have a DVD player, they brought one and then brought me DVDs. One AA friend from the city where I sobered up flew down to clean my apartment and another offered to help pay my phone bill.

During this time, I had to go to the dentist for root canal work. Then, after I returned home, my knee went out and I had to undergo arthroscopic surgery six weeks after the cancer surgery. I was limping with a cane and I couldn't lift my hands above my head because of the pain in my stomach from the cancer surgery. I tried to delay the knee surgery, but the chemotherapy had to start within a given period after the cancer surgery in order to have the most impact.

Chemotherapy was given to me in a place called the Chemo Co-op. I would go into the hospital on Monday at noon and they would hook me up to an IV, and I would take fifty hours of chemo. Then they would send me home on Wednesday afternoon. The chemo forced me to stay in bed from the Wednesday they released me to the following Monday or Tuesday. I was then allowed to recover and repeat the process the following week. At the Co-op, Anne-Margaret and AA friends came every day. And they came in droves. They brought books and magazines, food and incomparable warmth and companionship. Tom B. came every day with the papers and stayed most of the day. We would sit at the end of a row of chairs, four or five or more of us at a time. We called it the "talking and fooling around" section. Cancer areas can be very bleak.

"Who are all those guys?" asked my doctor, an oncologist for many years, during my weekly appointment. "When I met you, I said I was in AA. They are mostly from AA," I said. "Not Anne-Margaret?" he guessed. "No, not Anne-Margaret, but most of the rest." He said it was remarkable because often when people get cancer their friends don't know how to behave. "These guys don't know how to behave," I said. He said that wasn't what he meant, that often cancer patients' friends just disappeared. He said that the loyalty of my friends impressed him.

This course of chemo lasted for eight weeks, and I was given three weeks off before the chemo/radiation started. I was amazed at how quickly my strength returned. This was the beginning of November.

On November 24, 2004, Anne-Margaret developed meningitis, and she died December 4. Because of a set of very strange circumstances, and the tenacity of her disease, by the time I reached her she was already in a coma. They wouldn't allow me to hold her or kiss her good-bye. I was devastated. She had been so wonderful to me in every way. She had been calm through my tirades and patient during my tantrums. Everything seemed doable as long as I knew she was there. Now things were upside down.

My AA friends rallied again. They offered rides to the hospital in New Jersey so I could sit with her, then rides to the wake and the funeral. No one said "no" or "why," they just did it without my asking. They helped me through a set of impossibilities that I could not have gone through alone. I did not drink and I have not died, yet.

I am about halfway through my cancer treatments and the treatment from my AA friends continues. I miss Anne-Margaret constantly. I could never replace such a unique girl and the fact that she loved me surprises me still. But, of course, none of this would have happened without AA.

Shortly after being diagnosed with cancer, I was put in touch with a guy in AA who had experienced a similar situation. I asked him now that he had recovered, if it had changed him at all. "Oh, absolutely. Physically, morally, spiritually, definitely." "Really?" I said. "Oh yes. It took me almost six months to become the same selfish, self-centered bastard I'd always been." I wonder if the changes that have occurred in me will stick—more patience, more trust, less animosity, less suspicion—or will they fade away like my scar, leaving just a very faint trace.

I do not believe there is a loving God working in my life. I think the job has become too much for him. But I cannot live without some kind of spiritual life, so I pray to Anne-Margaret for help, and I have an inexhaustible amount of AA power to draw from for which I will be eternally grateful.

JOHN Q.
New York, New York

Only Love Has Meaning JUNE 1989
(Excerpt)

During my sobriety I have contracted the HIV infection (AIDS virus). The reason I am choosing to share my story is the certainty that I am not alone. With the great number of dually addicted people in AA (as well as their sexual partners), along with the long incubation period of the AIDS disease, I feel my experience might provide hope to someone out there who is hurting right now and feeling all alone.

When I had been sober for five years, my ex-boyfriend—whom I had not seen since 1983—advised me that he had tested positive for the AIDS virus. He was a recovering alcoholic and was abstinent from drugs during the two years that we were involved, though he has since gone back out there.

Imagine my consternation upon hearing this news. It took me quite a while to gather the courage and strength from my Higher Power to go for the AIDS test myself. I struggled with the insane, rampant thoughts running through my head. "I've been sober five years. I'm only twenty-seven. Oh my God, I'm going to die of a horrible disease. Who can I tell of this? I will be treated like a leper."

I prayed daily and shared my turmoil and fears with my sister and my two closest friends. These three gave me the strength to take the test, if only to put my mind to rest. After all, how could I be positive? I had had very few sexual encounters in sobriety and before sobriety. I have never used IV drugs. I have been sober for five years. I had not been with my ex-boyfriend for three whole years.

In 1986, I took the test. I waited a week for the results. "Turning it over" took quite an effort, but I continued to ask my Higher Power for help. The diagnosis was "HIV positive." I can't describe to you the despair and hopelessness I felt at the time. I thought my Higher Power had deserted me. I felt as if I was being punished, as if my childhood God had come back to haunt me. I had fully expected the results to be negative. Instead, I discovered I have had the virus in my body for anywhere from five to seven years.

My background in AA then began to serve me well. My first thought after the shock wore off was, "I need a support group." My Higher Power showed me then that he was taking care of me. Through the AIDS hotline, I had been referred to a meeting that had recently been started for IV drug users testing positive. I went to that meeting. It was in its second week. A drug counselor was running it. There was only the counselor, me, and a third person at this meeting. The third person was a girl like myself, five years sober, not an IV drug user, whose husband had also been a drug user and alcoholic years ago. We clung to each other during those first few months like two shipwrecked sailors. We shared our experiences, fears, hopes. We adapted the Twelve Steps and "How It Works" to our common bond, HIV positive. Since neither of us felt free to discuss this in an AA meeting, we needed the tools AA had given us to draw upon our strength and hope in living with this virus on a daily basis. The way of life we had discovered in AA kept us sober and sane in mind, body, and spirit, and we utilized these principles in coping with this virus.

What has emerged from all this pain, fear, and despair has been a gradual acceptance of the reality and uncertainty of my illness, as well as a gratitude for my Higher Power and a trust in him (at least most of the time, anyway). My Higher Power does provide for me as evidenced by the coincidence of a fellow AA member, a heterosexual woman, five years in sobriety, being at that particular meeting. Very few people are aware of my HIV status, but the people I have shared with besides my group have respected my anonymity and provided me with the love, care, and support I so desperately needed. I thought my Higher Power had deserted me and yet due to this program, and the way of life I had been practicing for the past seven years, my family was one hundred percent behind me. My two closest friends as well as my immediate family have shown me what true love and acceptance is all about. I have shared many tears with them as well as much laughter regarding this virus. You see, a person would never guess by my appearance that I carry this virus and, at times, it is very easy for me also to deny that reality. Humor at those times offsets for me the horrible reality of HIV.

Even though I sometimes despair of ever being intimate with someone again, I know through my past experiences in the program that when and if I am ready to share, my Higher Power will provide for me. I am single and I fully expected in my early thirties to experience motherhood and being a wife. My diagnosis as HIV positive changed that, for now, anyway. However, within every cloud is a silver lining and what I have learned from this virus is multifold.

The most important thing I learned is that life is too short. We must live only in today. We must live life to its fullest, giving it our best shot. For it is through living this way that we share the most important thing in life, which is love. It took a complete jolt like HIV to make me realize love is the only thing that has any meaning. I need people in my life today. My Higher Power speaks to me through people. Life is just too short to dwell upon past mistakes or to worry about future ones. Life is an experience meant to be lived, taking risks and knowing that the results are being cared for through our Higher Power. "Go with the passion." I am trying to keep my life simple and just to appreciate all of life, the pain as well as the joy. My life is not over because of this virus. As a matter of fact, I have become more aware of just what is important in my life and I have eliminated what is not.

I have maintained my sobriety and health due to the way of life AA teaches and I wanted to share my story with you in hopes that someone who is in my position will realize their Higher Power has not deserted them. He is there. He will give us the strength to deal with this on a daily basis like our alcoholism, one day at a time, if we just ask, and accept what he gives us.

ANONYMOUS

At My Age MARCH 2009

A little over a year ago, I was fired from my last job as a drug and alcohol counselor at a well-established treatment center. I was devastated: anger, frustration and denial were in full force as I was ushered out the door. I had been fired from the previous two positions I had held, and this was the charm! I felt worthless, bewildered and belittled. I felt that something was terribly wrong, but I couldn't persuade anyone to listen to me. At my AA group, all I got was a well-meant suggestion to take the Third Step. After 27 years of sobriety, I deserved better treatment than this, I thought.

I progressed in some sort of sickness that neither my wife nor I could pin down. I thought I was just depressed, and I had always found that one more meeting pretty well takes care of my depression. But not this time. I sank deeper and deeper and, finally, began to think suicidally, screaming to myself, "They'll all be sorry when I'm gone." As a last resort, I went to the hospital for evaluation.

While I was in the hospital, with my wife present and supportive through every single moment of the ordeal, I had both a stroke and a heart attack. The heart attack was the easier to deal with. The stroke, however, was a complete surprise to me, like nothing I had ever experienced. When I had recovered sufficiently, I was sent home with instructions that I was to be evaluated by a specialist. Upon following through, I was diagnosed with early onset Alzheimer's. My team of doctors ordered me not to seek employment. I became officially "disabled."

This was never supposed to happen to me! I came from a family filled with doctors and lawyers. I was a championship debater in college and a coach of national championship debaters. I had financed my way through college and graduate school on academic scholarships. I owned a computer programming business and had completed law school after staying sober for three years. I'd returned to teaching and become a school principal. Then, when I had gotten tired of teaching, I was certified as an alcoholism and drug counselor. Now, I could never work again. Ever!

Was this fair? Was this a part of the deal? Was I now relegated to a life of being "stupid, boring and glum"? I had a very difficult time reconciling my new status as terminally ill with my own mental self-image as "superman." My wife tried to reassure me, my group listened patiently, and ultimately I got very tired of trying to "figure it all out."

The last time I had felt this lost and alone was when I'd sobered up. I had been arrested in Lafayette, Louisiana, and strapped down in an isolation room until the police could figure out what to do with me. I knew as certainly as I know that I am typing these words that I heard the voice of my Higher Power clearly and distinctly saying, "Now are you willing to let me do this for you?" And since that moment, the moment I answered, "Yes," I had never—until now—questioned the will of God in my life.

I have been praying to that voice that I heard 27 years ago. I have also started getting phone calls from newcomers, who ask how they can possibly stay sober with everything going on in their lives. I recognize the anger and fear in their words, but realize they are trying to follow directions, just like me. They've mirrored back to me my own insecure fears and that has actually been helping me knuckle under and follow my own physicians' medical advice.

It took a long time for me to finally come back to the Third Step, as had been suggested when I first lost my job, but I'm grateful I did. It's not such a bad thing to have no answers. It's just a little scary.

JIM L.
Newton, Kansas

CHAPTER 2

MY GREATEST TEST SO FAR

Members who are deaf, blind, or otherwise disabled do whatever it takes to get to meetings, stay sober, and carry the message

Members who were differently abled before they came into the rooms, or who became deaf, blind, unable to walk, or otherwise physically challenged after they got sober, write about how they used the program to find peace with their limitations. Almost all of them had to take special actions and ask for help in order to keep hearing or reading the message, or to attend meetings. Most, at one point or another, felt the pangs of feeling "different." "We are all 'different' from other people, and that is what makes us alike," a deaf AA points out. Adds a fellow member confined to a wheelchair: "I'm still a drunk, whether I walk into these rooms or wheel in."

Speak Up! SEPTEMBER 2010

I was astounded to wake up one night, after I'd been sober for several years, with an insane dizziness and roaring in my head accompanied by a light-headedness on my right side. By morning I was thinking I must have had a stroke, but a visit with the doctor revealed that was not the case.

After many tests and examinations I learned that I had suffered a permanent hearing loss, probably due to age and heredity. Permanent. Millions of people suffer with hearing loss—my reaction, of course, was, "Why me?"

No fair. This should not have happened to me. I needed to be able to hear in AA meetings. I needed to be able to pick up on casual conversations in my midst. I needed to hear what people were saying at parties, in crowded restaurants, in stage performances; I needed to know what people were joking about, whispering about, crying about, laughing about. This was all gone.

Oh I could still hear, all right. Like many people with hearing loss, I heard muffled or garbled sounds, mumbled talk, annoying music, impossible telephone conversations, useless phone messages and spouses who turn the TV up too loud. In AA we learn that isolating is not good for us, but I wanted to retreat from the racket for the sake of my sanity.

My generic hearing aid let me hear conversations across the room, but not the ones I was trying for. In AA meetings I felt ignored, left out, different from. Occasionally someone would whisper into my entirely deaf right ear, leaving both of us frustrated and confused. When there was a burst of laughter, a chair scraping across the floor, or clapping, the magnified sound was unbearable.

In AA I had learned that acceptance is the key—as is action. I went to a foundation for the hard of hearing, where I took classes in speech reading ("lip-reading") and learned tactics that really helped, such as which seating arrangements could be most advantageous to the hearing-challenged, and how to direct people so that I could understand them.

An ear-nose-throat specialist told me where to go for a better hearing aid. I've also learned in AA to take direction, and in time I was fitted with the best hearing aid for my needs. The day the aid was placed in my only hearing ear, I returned to my car where the radio came on playing music—and I sat and cried at the astounding improvement in my hearing. I had never heard anything so beautiful in my life.

The hearing in my deaf ear will never return. Until technology catches up I will never know what direction sound is coming from, if a car with its engine running is close to me, what the punch line is or who is reading "How It Works." Travel by myself is difficult. But I can live with my disability by using the tools I have learned in AA and in the hearing group.

ANONYMOUS

An Inner Truth MAY 2007

I served in the United States Marines for ten years, and I was sure that it was the right career for me. Drinking was a pastime for many in my platoon and I fit right in. Then, in September of 1984, my life was turned upside down. One night, while returning from liberty, I was injured in a motorcycle accident that left me both physically and spiritually changed for the rest of my life. After eighteen months in the hospital and thirty-six surgeries, my right leg had to be amputated.

During my hospitalization, alcohol was not readily available, but I still found ways and means to acquire my old friend. I asked nurses and technicians to smuggle me bottles here and there, but there was never enough. But after being introduced to morphine and demerol, I required much less alcohol to keep "sane." By the time I left the hospital, I was not only an alcoholic, but an addict as well. Once released, I continued to drink alcoholically for the next ten years. The progression of the disease took me all the way to homelessness. My wife of seven years, who was also one of my nurses, could no longer take the pain of living with a very sick alcoholic and addict. She packed up my two children and left. Now alone, my drinking began to reach new limits. I was homeless—without a family, without a leg, and without a life. I didn't know which way to turn and suicide seemed an option worth investigating.

One night, I decided that I couldn't live with alcohol anymore—but I couldn't live without it. So, I devised a fail-proof plan to take my life. I took a vacuum hose and connected it to the exhaust of my truck, taped and sealed the windows, started the truck, finished my fifth (I wouldn't want to leave any behind), and prepared to die. I awoke the next morning in my truck, very sick, with an empty fifth, and very much alive. I looked at the gas gauge and there was still a quarter tank of gas left. The key was in the "on" position and the fail-proof plan had failed. The truck died during the night, and I didn't.

Somehow, a few months later, I ended up at an AA meeting sitting across the table from a man who had attempted suicide with a shotgun and blown his face off. He looked across the table at me and said, "Welcome," and then, "Boy, you look like crap." Coming from a man without a nose and a lot of facial damage, this statement stuck in my mind. A woman gave me a beginner token and a new way of life began to develop for me. I thought somehow I was different since I was physically handicapped, but I wasn't. You showed me that, wife or no wife, kids or no kids, legs or no legs, this program would work—if I could only be honest with myself.

Today, I have enjoyed nearly five years of recovery, and life is worth living. I joke around at meetings, saying it's easy for a man missing a leg to hit his knees in the morning. I thank God, the Fellowship, the Twelve Steps, and the woman who gave me that token—she held my hands the first few months, and let me know that love can move mountains (we've been married four years now). We might be different on the outside, but inwardly we are all the same.

TIM B.
Jasper, Indiana

Wills and Ways DECEMBER 2006

(From Dear Grapevine)

I am mentally ill and legally blind. I also have a physical disorder that prevents me from leaving the house. What I do have, however, is Alcoholics Anonymous, so I answer the central office phones from my home. I am grateful for nineteen years of sobriety.

MARY W.
Orange, California

The Hand of AA FEBRUARY 2000

My friends tore the covers off my Big Book, and then, with razor blades, cut the pages out of what was left. They were laughing about it. That book had been bought especially for me—it was soft cover, large print. Everyone was nervous (and a little guilty) about destroying a Big Book. It felt strange to dismantle the same book which had put so many lives back together. And yet, it had to be done to carry the message to one more alcoholic ... me.

I'm Maria and I'm an alcoholic. My friends from the Special Needs Committee were actually building a copy of the Big Book which I could pick up and read. In addition to my allergy to alcohol, I am allergic to the most common chemicals in everyday life, such things as cosmetics, perfumes, laundry detergent, bar soaps, chemicals in carpets, smoke (from a cigarette stubbed out an hour ago), and car exhaust. Yes, even the ink in a Big Book is poisonous to me.

At twelve years sober, I was diagnosed with another life-threatening disease, multiple chemical sensitivity. Upon inhaling the smallest hint of a proscribed substance my fingers begin to curl as if I have advanced arthritis, my esophagus swells and closes so that I can't swallow, my mind dims, dizziness sets in, and my strength slowly and completely disappears. I am powerless to stop it once it starts, nor can I easily avoid the cause. Only a small handful of people are affected by this condition, but the effect can be deadly.

"There'll come a time when you may want to kill yourself," my doctor said. "Many others have committed suicide or turned to drugs and alcohol." I had asked her to be completely honest. Prepare me for the worst so I can be ready, I had told her. She did. I'm the single mom of a wonderful four-year-old. I thought, What will happen to my daughter? I was scared to death.

I realized this could turn into the perfect excuse if I allowed it to—the perfect excuse to isolate, the perfect excuse to "medicate," the perfect excuse to insulate myself from reality just as I had done twelve years previously. I could drink away my fear and frustration, and who would say I was wrong! And who would know? I could no longer go outside. Car exhaust had already put me in the hospital. Almost no one came over to visit anymore. My four-year-old daughter was my primary caregiver, for God's sake! Who would know?

But a half-remembered thought began to take shape in my mind: "We just don't drink no matter what." But they didn't mean this. They couldn't have known about this! "We just don't drink no matter what." But living your life in a sterilized compartment? I sat and stared at my front door which had become a sort of hostile border. There were no guards except myself. But on the other side of that door was real danger. Close friends whom I had known for years were now the unwitting enemy. Could I tell my friends they must use a certain shampoo, change laundry detergent, not wear a certain perfume, and please, absolutely no make-up—or stay away? I had to watch my little girl, with straight-faced stoicism, give away her Christmas gifts because the dyes and chemicals might hurt her mommy.

"We just don't drink no matter what." I began to hate that phrase. Drinking or death became real options. I had grown up in an alcoholic family. I know from long and bitter experience how we work. We create chaos in our lives. We manufacture misery and blame it on "him" or "her" or "them" or "it," and I felt I had the Mother of All Excuses to go on a raging, no-looking-back bender. This was something I could blame on God and everybody else because I certainly had no part in this! I made legal arrangements with an old friend to take my daughter "should anything happen." I had almost decided to open that door and cross the border, walking into the world unprotected. But the hand of AA was there when I reached out.

I called our central office. It took time for them to realize the true problem and I can understand. At first glance it might seem like someone a little too sensitive to smoky meeting rooms or another drunk suffering from terminal uniqueness. After all, who could be allergic to practically everything on the planet?

But once they did realize that these were not fantastic claims, the hand of AA reached out in ways I had never thought to pray about. The Special Needs Committee kicked into high gear. I had prayed to have a meeting in my home once a week. They started two. They put me in touch with the "Tape Worm" program, and now I could share the unique frustration of being shut into my home with other alcoholics who are staying sober the same way. They managed to find an old fax machine which I could use to communicate with my doctor, my pharmacist, and the Environmental Protection Agency (I'm on a first name basis with people there!). It opened a world of communication I had felt was closed—slammed—in my face.

AA members open and read my mail to me, otherwise I'd have no idea what my bills are. They go shopping and refill prescriptions. They covered my carpet with thick plastic so the mold and fibers stay in the carpet. Perhaps most important of all, my daughter does not have to join me in my disease. Occasionally an AA member will take her out into the open where she can enjoy being four years old again. These are the practical miracles which my Higher Power has brought through the Special Needs Committee. Though these activities may not be strictly AA-related, they addressed real sources of fear and depression for me, two emotions I always felt were excellent reasons to drink. But through reliance on my Higher Power and the support of the Special Needs Committee, no matter what has happened, I have not had a drink.

I have been trying to think of a way to end this piece, but there really isn't one. Both my diseases are for life. There is no cure, no remission, and to succumb to either one of them could easily mean my death. But there is hope. My Higher Power found a way, even now, to improve my life far beyond what I dreamed was possible. I have learned that I have passed the initial hurdle to become the first person in my state acknowledged as having this disease. Help may soon come to not just myself, but others who, until now, were not even recognized as being sick.

Oh yes, my Big Book? The pages my friends cut out with that razor are now safely sealed in plastic sleeves and placed in a three-ring binder. I have my Big Book back, I have my sobriety, and even some serenity. All because someone made sure that the hand of AA was there. I have a life back.

MARIA

No Need to Be Alone OCTOBER 1990
(Excerpt)

We are all "different" from other people, and that is what makes us alike. For me, I never knew what it was like not to be different. Born with a severe hearing impairment that slid into a profound hearing loss as the years went by, I had no trouble identifying with speakers who spoke about being "different" from other people.

What of my deafness? Well, I have to sit close to the speaker of course. And as sponsee or sponsor, the telephone just won't do; I have to see your face to lip-read. This means a lot of miles on the car, but I think face-to-face conveys a lot more of our special kind of love than the telephone can do.

I'm very aware of the fact that there are virtually no other deaf or hard-of-hearing people in the meetings, but I no longer feel different, as you people won't let me feel that way. Instead, I've convinced the intergroup office that a TDD machine is necessary. Maybe a special meeting, along with someone who speaks sign language, will bridge the gap and penetrate a few other iron walls out there. I look forward to the day when some shaking alcoholic, with a thing in his ear, is going to peek into a church basement. I want to shake his hand vigorously and tell him or her to come on in. There is no need to be alone again.

RICK S.
Ottawa, Ontario

An Important Secret JULY 2001

(From Dear Grapevine)

I have been sober in this Fellowship for sixteen years, having come in for the second time in 1984. I'm now thirty-eight years old. Ten years ago, while in college, I fell down some icy stairs. I can no longer walk and am considered physically challenged.

The fact that I'm in a wheelchair does not give me a reason to drink. I let my Higher Power and AA help keep me sober. I still can go to AA meetings, even the ones with stairs—people just carry me down. I went to any lengths to drink, so I will do what it takes to stay sober. I'm no different from anyone else, except for the physical part. I'm still a drunk, whether I walk into these rooms or wheel in.

We can always come up with a reason to drink. The secret is, how many reasons can we come up with to stay sober? I believe anyone can stay sober if they trust, work, learn, and seek help from a Higher Power. Mine is God. All I have to do is ask.

JOHANNA W.
Topeka, Kansas

Blindsided APRIL 2010

Marking my 30th anniversary of being sober was for me most humbling. I had been through the death of both my parents, the loss of a career, two divorces and several major moves. Never once did I pick up that drink. Little did I know at the time that a few months later, I would face one of my greatest tests so far.

In July of 2004 I had surgery on my right eye to reduce pressure caused by severe glaucoma.

The surgery failed, and so the ophthalmologist ordered a process called "needling" to open the scar. This too failed, and I was sent to yet another specialist. This doctor asked a rather strange question about my heritage. I understand now that I have a rare birth defect known as optical neuropathy, which affects many Danes. I have subsequently endured multiple eye tests and slowly have lost all but 20 percent of my sight.

Four years have now passed, and others say I have adapted quite well to my blindness. Life is challenging (a new politically correct word for my age in life). I have learned to care for myself: cooking, washing clothes, gardening, painting my house and paying bills; as well as building gates, bird houses and candle holders. I rely heavily on sound and listen to my talking computer to handle my paperwork and banking.

Life is good and I thank God for recordings of music, books-on-tape and the news. I do not watch television and I do not go out at night. I walk most everywhere in my hometown; this includes meetings, the post office, the grocery store and the pharmacy. I have little defense against two-ton cars, motorcycles, buses, trucks, bicycles or skateboards.

Yes, life as a recovering alcoholic is even more of a challenge to-day than it was four years ago. As a blind person I hear extra keenly, and therefore all side conversations at meetings are bothersome. I cannot identify the speaker except by voice. I do not know who someone is when he or she touches me; people have to announce in a clear voice who they are.

I am not invisible; I still exist as a human being even though I am blind, and I do know the sound of my friends' voices. But it is still helpful to me when others announce themselves before they approach me, and when they don't invade my space.

I am not asleep in meetings; I am just quiet and listening to what is being said.

I have no more cause to drink now than ever. I only add blindness to my list of things I absolutely have to accept. There is no other choice. I accept blindness as I do my alcoholism—thanks to AA and y'all.

O.P.
Santa Rosa, California

PART TWO
EMOTIONAL ADVERSITY

CHAPTER 3
LIFE WILL KEEP ON HAPPENING

Seeking help for their fear, anxiety, depression, or mental illness helped these alcoholics move forward in recovery

"I had lost all hope of my life getting any better," writes a member who finds himself deep in depression at 10 years sober. "I had lost my faith in God, and my pride would not allow me to return to AA and ask for help." Another writes that after 23 years in the program without a drink, she stills gets into dark emotional places where suicide looks like a reasonable option. There can be deep trepidation in asking for help, especially when one has double digits of sobriety. A member quotes co-founder Dr. Bob in one of his last talks to the Fellowship: "Don't think that because I'm fifteen-and-a-half years sober I'm any farther from the next drink than any of you." The stories in these pages are about seeking help for these emotional problems. Sometimes the help comes from outside, sometimes through the Steps, but it's always by working the AA program and staying sober that AAs are able to find it.

Unreasonable Fears JULY 2010

Fear was my constant companion when I was still drinking. I had panic attacks. I couldn't deal with stress. I was afraid to live— and I couldn't master suicide. The fear was so great at one point that I took off work for a month. I couldn't function, and I was still drinking to try to control the fear.

When I got sober I was still very afraid. However, as I worked the Steps, I found the fear dissipating. It wasn't totally gone, but I could function. My sponsor suggested I do a fear inventory. I would concentrate on that part of my illness that was still bothering me. This was great. It was OK to write down that I was afraid of spiders and couldn't even get close enough to one to kill it. I had lived in California all my life but was getting really panicky that an earthquake might hit.

I was afraid of success and of failure. When I finished the inventory and gave it away, I felt more relief.

As the years went on and I stayed sober, life brought me new fears to deal with and old fears that hadn't yet been removed. When each one surfaced I shared about it. I was no longer ashamed to admit how afraid I was of many very irrational situations and things. Other people seemed to relate and admitted they had fears, too.

I saw that fear was a character defect, so I modified my Seventh Step Prayer. After "remove every single defect of character," I added, "and every unreasonable fear."

Learning how to cope with fear has been a great blessing of my 20 years of sobriety. The most important thing I do is to continue to work the Steps.

JEANNE L.
Brea, California

Many Do Recover APRIL 2004
(From Dear Grapevine)

I've been sober now for fourteen years. My first sponsor told me that he couldn't stay sober until he was diagnosed with bipolar depression and got help. I myself have schizophrenia, an anxiety disorder, and major depression. I used to work the Steps over and over, and still I was an emotional basket case. I finally became suicidal and was put in the hospital. God only knows why I didn't drink. The point is my sponsor and I are both sober now and doing well since we got the extra help we needed along with the AA program. If reading this enlightens one person and helps him or her, I feel it was worth writing.

ANONYMOUS
New York, New York

Living Life Forward OCTOBER 2005

Let me begin by saying that I am not one who has drifted away from Alcoholics Anonymous. I have a loving Higher Power and a sponsor, I have an active service position in my home group, I attend several meetings a week, I sponsor women, and I've been working the Steps of Alcoholics Anonymous since the beginning to the best of my ability. That is why I was baffled when, at nineteen years sober, I became leveled by depression.

I had experienced bouts of depression since I was a young woman, but marriage, a family, and active drinking took the edge off until I got to AA. Then, from March 2003 to March 2004, my mother died, my two twelve-year-old dogs died, I had an accident with my horse, and I experienced heart problems. By October, I had hit a dark bottom, with all the symptoms of depression: fatigue, anger, acute sadness, sleep problems, and a sense of hopelessness. I was losing interest in the things I loved doing.

I kept thinking, If I just work the Steps deeper, if I do more service, if I talk about it in meetings, pray more, exercise more, eat right, I'll be okay. Unfortunately, this was not the case.

My sponsor had become very busy in her own life and was pretty much inaccessible at a time I was desperate. Then I remembered that the Big Book says we have to place our dependence on God, not people, and I heard in meetings "in our desperation is God's opportunity." Finally, one morning I got on my knees and surrendered to God, simply saying, "God, I am powerless over this illness, please send help." The next day, I got an email out of the blue from a former sponsor who had moved out of state. I hadn't intended to resume our relationship, but she knew me better than anyone else, so I wrote back telling her I was having a difficult time.

As she usually did, she asked me to do a Fourth Step, which I emailed to her. My depression must have been pretty obvious because she called me at 3:00 A.M. to see if I was okay. She suggested very strongly that I contact a doctor I knew through AA; he in turn directed me to another doctor in AA who was knowledgeable about depression. Within forty-eight hours, I was sitting in her office, pouring out my story.

I'm so grateful to our Big Book and the insights it shares with respect to seeking outside professional help. I was referred to a psychiatrist for proper diagnosis. I would like to say that I was given a magic pill to solve my ills, but God has other ideas. I had adverse reactions to my initial treatment, but meanwhile I reached out to some men and women I had met in an old-timers' meeting. They were able to share their experience, strength, and hope about how some of them had dealt with depression in long-term sobriety. These men and women lifted me up and helped me see how God

is carrying me right now. I have been given hope, love, and acceptance beyond my wildest dreams.

One day, I was having a horrible reaction to medication and I
didn't get a chance to share during the meeting. One of the members took a group conscience vote to extend the meeting so that I
could get their help. Not one person left. They practiced what the
Big Book says about giving our brother or sister alcoholics first aid.
What an example of the power of the AA program. It was an incredible example of love.

The answers aren't yet clear how I will be treated for my second illness, but my hope today is that I will recover, and what once
seemed like a dark hole will be another opportunity to trust in
God's outcome. I ask God, "What do you want me to learn from
the depression?" because I know from my journey in sobriety that
God always takes what I perceive as a problem and brings some
good out of it, especially if it will help another suffering alcoholic. I
also know I have to trust that the gifts will be given and the lessons
learned on God's timetable, not mine.

It's funny how life is lived forward—and understood backward.

PAM C.
Vail, Arizona

Life—It Happens MAY 2005

(Excerpt)

I n February, I celebrated thirty years of sobriety, and in March,
I turned sixty years old. Both celebrations would have been
inconceivable for me on that miserable day when I made the call to
AA and said those now familiar words, "My name is Joe, and I'm
an alcoholic."

I'm really happy that I was led into the Steps right away. As the result of doing the Fourth and Fifth Steps in my third month, I experienced the beginnings of the spiritual awakening that I believe has kept me sober all these years. For me, the greatest promise of the program is the one in the Twelfth Step. It tells me I will have a spiritual awakening as the result of the Steps. I know I need that awakening to have a chance to stay sober.

I hear a lot of people say at meetings that it keeps getting better in sobriety. That hasn't been the case with me. Different, yes. Sober, yes. But life has kept on happening. I had a terrific struggle with a social anxiety disorder that started in my third year and lasted for about nine years. Some time after I recovered from that, I was hit with a chronic depressive disorder that I still struggle with. My wife of many years returned to drinking after seventeen years, and I spent some time raising our two boys as a single parent.

But sobriety continues. The measure of my sobriety isn't the distance between now and the last drink—the measure of my sobriety is the distance between now and the next drink. And I know how to keep that distance: the Steps, trying to stay connected to a Higher Power, and working with others. Coincidentally, a few weeks ago I was listening to a tape of one of Dr. Bob's last talks. In that talk he said at one point, "Don't think that because I'm fifteen-and-a-half years sober I'm any farther from the next drink than any of you."

A few months ago, I tapped into a survey on my computer. The survey said it would help to determine how long I would live. I'm not sure why it attracted my attention, but I went on to complete the questions about lifestyle, illness, family history, and so on. The result was that I could live to be ninety. That brought a chuckle to this one day at a time alcoholic.

There's a kind of symmetry to the whole thing: I spent the first thirty years making a mess of the life I was given, the next thirty trying to figure out this simple program, and now I can try in the last thirty to loosen up, let life happen, and try to have a little fun.

But if my experience is worth anything, it tells me that life will keep happening, as long as it lasts. There will be ups and downs, and spiritual progress and setbacks. But at the end of each day as I extend my sobriety past age sixty, I hope that I can say a short prayer of gratitude for another day of sobriety. Anything else good that happens is a bonus.

JOE B.
White Rock, British Columbia

A New Perspective FEBRUARY 2006
(From Dear Grapevine)

D espite twenty-three years of sobriety, I still experience times when I feel like I want to end my life. The section on depression in the October (2006) issue gave me great hope. I was thinking that I had to keep this problem to myself. After reading the articles, I realized, once more, that I don't have to be alone with this illness, and that taking a psychiatrist's prescription doesn't make me a hypocrite in AA. I am grateful to the members who contributed to the section. They put this issue into perspective for me.

LINDIE B.
Redondo Beach, California

Falling Apart on the Inside

APRIL 2005

(Excerpt)

In my tenth year of recovery, I found myself well-grounded in the program. I was active, my support system was strong, and my life was good. I had a growing career in local television as a studio engineer. Financially, I had more than I could ask for. In fact, I had recently purchased the first new vehicle I had ever owned. My support group consisted of one very close friend. This was a man older than me, whom I had known since I first entered recovery.

It would be foolish of me to try to justify my reasons for drifting from AA. Simply put, I began to substitute exercise for meetings. I joined a gym and started running on a regular basis. The more I did, the more I enjoyed it, the more I wanted to do. My ego said, you have ten years, you don't need meetings every day; and my vanity kept telling me how good I looked. I listened.

One Saturday afternoon, I returned home from the gym and my neighbor told me my friend had suddenly passed away. The shock of the loss was devastating. I could think of nothing but to go to a meeting. However, once there, my pride would not allow me to show my pain or ask for help. My disease had begun to flare up, and my support system was crumbling. I continued to attend meetings in the weeks to come, but only in body. I stayed to myself, spoke very little, arrived late, and left early. My pride kept telling me I was okay—I didn't feel like drinking, I didn't need any help, I had ten years without a drink. I was in AA and alone. Eventually, I stopped going to meetings altogether.

As time passed, I was consumed with my job and my workout program, all the while growing more and more isolated. I worked alone most of the time, and did not notice that I was becoming more distant with the people at the gym. I had no circle of friends, and my only family was my mother, who, like me, enjoyed isolation.

Time passed and due to corporate consolidation, my job was being phased out. I knew it for some time, but did nothing to seek work elsewhere. I refused to accept the things I could not change. In May of last year, as a last resort to save my job, I resigned my position with the company. I believed my resignation would draw corporate attention to the foolish manner in which an individual was running the department and, after seeing this, they would certainly acknowledge my value to the company and, in their infinite wisdom, create a new position suitable for someone with my vast qualifications.

Unemployed and with no income, the situation grew worse. Through the summer, I managed a few part-time jobs. There were several good opportunities for full-time employment, but because of my attitude and the prolonged isolation, I could not get past the interviews. I knew I needed help, but my pride would not allow me to ask anyone. I continued to justify my control by telling myself that as long as I didn't drink I was alright. "I'm not drinking, so why do I need AA?"

As the holidays drew closer, the part-time work began to dry up. My depression grew to the point where, by Christmas, I was considering suicide as the only option. I had lost all hope of my life getting any better. I had lost my faith in God, and my pride would not allow me to return to AA and ask for help. I went to church for the first time in years, hoping that I would find something there that would rekindle my hope and faith, but it was no use. I sat in the back, spoke to no one, and left without even being noticed. Finally, after Christmas, I returned to my local clubhouse.

I did not return with any humility. On the contrary, I was arrogant and angry that my disease had gotten the best of me, that I could not do this on my own. It angered me to see the laughter and the fellowship in the room. On the outside, I was bitter and deliberately keeping a physical barrier between me and the happiness; inside, I was crying. I stood in the back—anxious, nervous, overwhelmed with emotions, fearful that someone would approach me and try to talk to me or, God forbid, offer me their hand in fellowship. I was afraid of being touched. As the gavel hit the table to announce the beginning of the meeting, I headed toward the door. I turned and ran head on into my sponsor, the only person I could never lie to. He grabbed my hand and, placing it in his, looked me squarely in the eye and said, "Where the hell have you been?" The best way to describe him is a cross between Santa Claus and Dirty Harry. He has the compassion of a saint with the tenacity of a drill sergeant. He was smiling with a gleam in his eye. I knew I could not avoid his question. His look became serious and he asked if I had drunk. When I told him that I hadn't, his smile returned, and he said, "I have your thirteen-year medallion. You want it?" I said no, and explained that I didn't feel I deserved to celebrate this anniversary in AA. Still holding my hand, he said, "Cliff, you can't do this on your own." I was falling apart inside. I managed to make him a promise that if I were still in AA in September, we could celebrate my fourteen years together. He laughed, let go of my hand, and took his seat. I, on the other hand, headed for the door. I made it to the coffee pot, where, out of habit, I stopped for a cup. That pause was enough. I returned and forced myself to sit through my first AA meeting in almost three years.

The next two weeks were difficult. I had to force myself each day to make a meeting. As the days passed, though, it became easier. I saw friends I hadn't seen and I began to feel more at ease. God was doing for me what I could not do for myself. I wanted to reach out to people, but I could not. My fear, pride, ego, my disease would not allow me to. AA reached out to me. No one at the gym, at work, in my neighborhood, or even in church had ever put their hand out to me. In AA, it happened every day.

One day, on my way to a meeting, the insanity of my life was spinning around in my head. The anxiety, fear, and insecurity over my living situation all combined to take over my thoughts. Anger, remorse, and self-pity all bottled up inside me, making me feel physically ill. Suddenly, everything went quiet. It was so sudden and shocking, I stopped in my tracks. My first thought was of my friend who had passed on years earlier. I saw him in my mind's eye, walking the same path I was taking, with his Irish gait and his smile, and I started to laugh out loud. After I regained my composure, I noticed how warm it was outside, a spring-like day, and how loud the birds were. A sense of well-being filled me. I cannot to this day explain what happened, but I knew everything was going to be alright. At the meeting, a newcomer introduced himself. I sought him out after the meeting and offered to be his sponsor. He became the first of three that I would begin sponsoring again. This action was not new to me. I had done this many times in the past, but it was new at this time in my recovery.

Today, my living situation is slowly returning to some stability. I know that a new chapter has once again started in my life—a chapter that has no ending, a chapter that I did not write, but a chapter with many characters. I have not felt alone in months now, even when I'm by myself. I have once again opened my heart to the God of my understanding. He is with me, and so is my friend.

CLIFF P.
Trenton, New Jersey

An Outside Issue? OCTOBER 2005

August 11, 2003, was my five-year sobriety anniversary. Less than one month before this, I voluntarily entered the hospital with a plan to kill myself.

I'd known for months that something wasn't right. I'd worked the AA program to the best of my ability, but I just kept getting more and more miserable. It was never about wanting to drink. It was about wanting the pain to end. I've since been diagnosed with a major depressive disorder, and I take medicine in order to keep it in remission.

Some would say that depression is an outside issue. I disagree. I can't begin to tell you how many fellow alcoholics have shared their experience, strength, and hope with me about their "grave emotional and mental disorders" since I began talking about my experiences. I knew I couldn't keep this a secret because I might drink again from the shame.

I am grateful to be alive today and to be sober. I am grateful I was able to ask for help, no matter how far down I had to go before I could do it. I am grateful to my Higher Power and to every kind person who let me know in some way that I'm loved. Once again, AA has saved me.

KELLY H.
Newport News, Virginia

CHAPTER 4

NOT IN MY LIFEBOAT: WHEN LOVE AND TOLERANCE FAIL US

Letting go of resentments and judgments about fellow AAs

AAs in this chapter write about how they've had to work at maintaining serenity in the face of prejudice, intolerance and disrespect from a fellow member—or how they've struggled to let go of resentments they themselves feel toward other members of the Fellowship. "I am not so naive as to believe that there are no AA members who have ... prejudices," writes an African-American AA, struggling with feeling different and hearing an actual racial slur from another member. "There are such members, but their ideals and ideas do not alter the basic tenets of the Twelve Steps and Twelve Traditions of Alcoholics Anonymous." Likewise, all of the difficulties these AAs had with other members only served to shed light on how the program should be lived.

The Watering Hole SEPTEMBER 2003

The noon meeting was, as usual, packed. I sat in my regular spot—dead in the middle of the nonsmoking side of the room. It was a few minutes before 12:00, with everyone buzzing, settling in with their coffee and ashtrays. Two men walked in and moved toward the last seats available: the front of the smoking section. At first, all I could see was their backs, but as they turned to sit I recognized one of them. Let's call him Mike. A few years earlier, Mike had worked in one of the divisions I oversee for a large organization. As the division manager, I had given his supervisor authorization to fire him for behaviors that could arguably be typical of many alcoholics. Mike's departure was viewed as "good riddance" by management and labor alike.

While working for us, he had made the acquaintance of another staff member I'll call Bob. Bob had come from a small upstate town after being honorably discharged from military service. He was a young man trying to make his way in the big city, but with no special skills. However, unlike Mike, Bob was an excellent worker. He had a really good attitude and willingness to work long and hard. In other words, he was a dream come true to an employer of unskilled blue-collar labor. His supervisor and co-workers shared a high opinion of him. Ironically, that high opinion would lead to a very strange turn of events.

The fact is, unskilled labor became a scarce resource in the 1990s. Low unemployment rates kept employers competing for workers, particularly ones with good habits. In an effort to hang onto Bob, we decided to give him a promotion and a rather substantial raise in pay. I still remember how happy his supervisor was when I told him we could do this. He couldn't wait to give the news to Bob, which he did the next afternoon.

If I thought his supervisor was happy, it paled in comparison to Bob's reaction. He was downright ecstatic—so happy and surprised, he asked if he could leave early. Apparently, he was so overwhelmed he was weak. With a warm, fuzzy feeling, his supervisor told him to go home and enjoy the day. I'll wish forever that I could take that decision back. We never saw Bob again.

The police later determined that when Bob got home, he discovered two men, later identified as Mike and a drifter, robbing his apartment. Mike eventually confessed, claiming that he had expected Bob to be at work, and that the drifter killed Bob—strangling him with his bare hands. Mike got a few years and the drifter got life. Poor Bob got forever. He must have been in terror as he died. To this day, a memorial plaque dedicated by his co-workers hangs in his work area. I had the task of telling his parents the circumstances; I wanted them to know how much we had liked their son.

Now here was Mike at an AA meeting, with his back to me. It would be so easy. I felt the rage starting up inside. My face must have turned colors. I had felt anger in meetings before, but never like this. I started to plot how I could get a shot at Mike. I knew that physically I could take him. Then a really strange thought hit me: I am at the watering hole.

On the African savannah, water is scarce. At the watering hole, predator and prey completely change behavior. Zebras and lions take turns: the zebras drink without fear of the lions and the lions drink without thought of eating the zebra, often within a few yards of each other. These primitive animals instinctively know that the watering hole is for their common good. If the zebras can't drink, eventually the lions will starve. The watering hole is a sacred resource available to everyone. No creature may take it away from any other, or eventually all will be lost. You could say that their common welfare comes first.

That thought and all of its implications allowed me to let go of some real anger that day. I never acknowledged Mike's presence. I think he saw me out of the corner of his eye, but he refused to look at me. After the meeting, he and his friend had the meeting secretary sign what I believe was one of those prove-it-to-the-court papers, and they immediately left. I never saw Mike again. But the realization that AA is there for our common good became cemented in me. When I saw the parallels between the meeting and the watering hole, I could never look at AA the same way again. Every person trying to gain sobriety meets the Third Tradition, whether or not they meet with my approval. No matter what may have occurred between us outside the rooms, it must remain outside. I must always remember that AA is the watering hole.

STEPHEN T.
Harrisburg, Pennsylvania

Shake My Hand DECEMBER 2010
(From Dear Grapevine)

I have found myself having trouble setting my boundaries in the rooms of AA. As a woman, when I offer my hand instead of a hug, I wish the men in the rooms would respect that. A lot of women in the program have been abused physically and no one knows what kind of day we are having mentally—a hug may trigger some bad memories. Don't make us feel bad by saying, "Oh, come on, what is this? Give me a hug."

I would like to suggest this as a topic. Thanks for listening.

JACQUI C.

Memoirs of a Black AA AUGUST 1985

(Excerpt)

I have found AA to be the way out for me. I have not come to this conclusion lightly. Of course, I had to take the First Step, admitting that I was powerless over alcohol. But I also had to accept the fellowship in an association that is dominated by whites and puts emphasis on a spiritual awakening. There was little problem in my accepting the spiritual basis of the AA program, since I had received a strong religious foundation at home and recognized the importance of a Higher Power in my life.

The race question was different. I am not so naive as to believe that there are no AA members who have racial, religious, and social prejudices and are willing to give vent to their feelings. There are such members, but their ideals and ideas do not alter the basic tenets of the Twelve Steps and Twelve Traditions of Alcoholics Anonymous. Bill W., AA's co-founder, emphasized that these members would not be a menace to AA but would serve as teachers, forcing those who would live up to the principles of AA to cultivate patience, tolerance, and humility. Bill saw AA as "a society of alcoholics in action," carrying a message that was just as important for survival to those who carried the message as to those who would receive it.

A few years earlier, I had decided to stop drinking and join AA. I was going to meetings and maintaining a semblance of sobriety. I was not happy, and I looked upon AA members as a group of people whom I would tolerate, though I really did not feel comfortable in their presence. One night, one of the white members made a racial slur directed at me. I felt hurt. When I left the meeting, I felt the whole exercise was useless, so I went to the nearest bar and proceeded to get drunk. At that period in my life, I thought that my failure to succeed in AA was the result of the insult of one white member and the coldness of the group. I realize now that was merely a rationalization on my part, so I could continue to drink. Today, I will let no one stand in the way of my sobriety.

I am hoping that many other black alcoholics will begin to see the advantages of trying Alcoholics Anonymous. I have been concerned about seeing too few "brothers and sisters" attending AA meetings. Does this mean that few blacks need the benefits of the program? Decidedly not. Does this mean that the black alcoholic is not seeking treatment and is willing to bear the pain? One only needs to go through the hospitals and treatment centers to find those who are seeking relief from the pain of the disease. Yet it seems that when the pain is gone and the health is returning, nothing else is done to get to the root of the problem.

I have asked many of my black friends whose drinking has caused and is causing problems: Why not try AA? The answers they give are sadly similar to those I once used: They have the willpower to quit when they want to; they would not feel comfortable telling their problems in an integrated group; if they wanted spiritual awakening, they would go to church, where people really understand the Higher Power; they are never going to get anything out of AA, so why waste the time with boring meetings?

I had used those same rationalizations regularly before I met my moment of truth. I learned that people with the same problem will ignore the question of race when they are truly intent on solving that problem. "Jim's Story" in the Big Book of Alcoholics Anonymous clearly shows this, as white members in AA helped Jim start a group for blacks during that period of strict segregation. If an alcoholic, because of a fear of racial rejection, avoids a group that could save his or her life, that person is either a fool or has a suicide wish, I believe.

Before I left this treatment center, I met a young black man who had been sober for a year. He was happy with his accomplishments; and well he should be, for he was (and still is) faced with all the obstacles—poverty, disease, unemployment, rejection, fear—that other young black men and women are faced with in many segments of this society and try to surmount with alcohol. This young man was keenly aware that even if a solution to the race problem came, that if opportunities for education, employment, and equal status were presented to him immediately, he could not take advantage of that progress if he was not sober and freed of the grip of alcoholism.

I reflected on his status and that of other alcoholics who are recovering. I knew in my heart that if I wanted to be effective in my community—as I have so arrogantly proclaimed in the past—I must first help myself. The road to recovery is long. I have taken the first step of the thousand miles; now, I must take each step one day at a time.

C. H.
Jackson, Mississippi

Sinking Fast MAY 2010

I had been sober for 13 years and was going through one of the worst dry drunks I had ever experienced. I had just moved out west to my hometown, where all the ghosts and reminders of my drinking career and failures in life were waiting. Successfully avoiding a return to this city for the last 20 years, my strategy was not to have to face my family—their questions, their dysfunction, their humanness.

But here I was back again, out of work and out of a relationship. I'd lost my home and my business, and was hating it. It wasn't long before my engine was pulling a long string of resentments and judgments.

Everyone here in AA was an idiot. They didn't run the meetings like I was used to. They were too large. People shared about everything under the sun except the program of recovery in AA. No one laughed at my sense of humor. I was something, at my home group back east. Here, I don't think they knew who I thought I was, and I was sinking fast.

I began to contemplate another drink, maybe on a trip some-where, where no one would know. I didn't want anything to do with my family. They could all take a flying leap, followed closely by me. I knew I wasn't being all that smart. I remembered the part in the Big Book where the number one offender for returning to alcohol was resentments, but I didn't seem to have the power to get that train back on a better track.

One night, in a moment of desperation, I got down on my knees and remembered a prayer an old sponsor had given me. It said, "God, help me be of service ... to something or someone ...." I knew intuitively it was the answer.

The next day I got an unexpected phone call from an AA who wanted to go to a meeting. My prayer ran through my head and I agreed. After the meeting, I found myself being drawn to the back of the room, where a newcomer was scanning a list of temporary sponsors. I asked him if he would like to go for a coffee sometime and he agreed. As I found out, he was living at the Salvation Army with basically only the clothes on his back.

His wife and son had committed suicide recently and he was in bad shape—much worse than my situation. But he seemed ea-ger to understand the program and work the Steps. I knew God at that moment had chosen this situation for both of us to help each other. One thing led to another, and before long there were five of us going through the Steps together, just like when AA started. I was passing along my experience going through the work, just like other members who had shown me. I was grateful again, and my attitude started to change. I wondered if my newcomer would stick to the Step study, since he was very new in sobriety, but he showed up every week reliably. He wanted it, and he was showing me that if I wanted to get back on track, I had to want it too.

Months passed, and before long he was getting involved in ser-vice, helping drunks and other people in need. He became em-ployable, and after a few years, met a like-minded woman and got married. Today I don't see him very much, but I hear through the grapevine that he is well and actively involved in service. I look back and wonder if God used me to help this guy so that in return, I could get myself out of a serious jam.

I know I make an impact on other people who are new in the program, because I know the impact other people made on me. I hope I always remember this lesson.

CLIFF A.
Edmonton, Alberta

Another Story JANUARY 2004
(From Dear Grapevine)

Many times, I have had at least a portion of my story told in Grapevine, but never more eloquently as that told in "Don't Idealize AA" (September 2003). In meetings around the country, I often have had the thought, Where's the love I hear about in Grapevine? AA and my Higher Power got me sober, but it certainly wasn't because of a loving, caring community.

At one point, my wife was confined to bed and a wheelchair for two years, and I never heard a comment of either sympathy or concern, let alone love. When, at eight and a half years of sobriety, I quit attending meetings, not a single person asked why or contacted me. The five years in recovery since have consisted of reading Grapevine, and I've never been more happy, joyous, and free.

I've no doubt some members will rush to defend the Fellowship from such heresy, probably proclaiming that I must be unlovable. But I think their efforts might be better spent in doing both a personal and a group inventory to find out how they stack up in the reaching-out department.

ANONYMOUS
Check, Virginia

A Plea for Love and Tolerance

APRIL 1999 *(From Dear Grapevine)*

Imagine going to your home group and being avoided by people with ten or more years of sobriety because they heard you volunteer your time with people with AIDS. Just for a moment, think about what it might be like for a gay man just getting sober to hear someone with "good sobriety" put down gays, blacks, and women. I've been there. I've heard the disparaging remarks about gays and lesbians—in a straight meeting where "love and tolerance is our code." The only reason I stuck around was because I was a hopeless drunk and I had nowhere else to go.

Several years later, I still have a lot of trouble with acceptance. I can't quite accept hearing people with so-called good sobriety tout the Big Book and then put down gays and other minorities in the same sentence. Thank God, there are gay meetings on Long Island, where I can go a couple of times a week and know I'm not going to hear some form of hatred directed at me or others.

The gay meetings I go to are open to anyone. If you show up, you won't hear derogatory remarks being made. And please don't assume that we dilute the message by having a "specialty" meeting. Our primary purpose is to stay sober and help other alcoholics to achieve sobriety.

JIM S.
Hauppauge, New York

At Home in a Home Group

FEBRUARY 1991 *(From Dear Grapevine)*

Having a home group has been very important to me. It has also been a growing experience. I'm two years sober, and still feel very unique at times, but the members of my home group have helped me in my recovery. I only regret that I have not been very grateful for this at times.

In just two years, I've seen people in AA go through all sorts of adversity. Relationship problems, marital problems, anger, resentment, and suicide. But it seems like we always stick together no matter how tough it gets.

There have been several occasions where I've wanted to leave my home group. I've been very fortunate, though, and have always had an understanding member to talk it over with me. These people have saved my life, not by feeding my resentment or anger but by telling me that it was normal to feel the way I do at times. This reassured me that I was not unique, and that everyone in the group goes through these things. Thank God for the home group and AA.

D. L.
Roanoke, Virginia

Babies Are Not Us? MARCH 2010

(From Dear Grapevine)

As a single mother of three, it is often hard to get to meetings. Sadly, when I do get to one, the hypocrisy frustrates and angers me.

I just came back from a breakfast meeting in Quebec, where I went with my 15-month-old son. My choice was to either bring him with me or miss the meeting.

"This is a closed meeting," a member said to me, darting a look at my baby, sitting quietly in his stroller. Where is this patience and tolerance that AA is constantly pushing?

Today I really needed a meeting. As I sat listening to members sharing, I was reminded of how fortunate I was to have found the rooms of AA once again four years ago. It's too bad that some old-timers, like the woman who made it clear that I'm not welcome if I have my baby with me, have gotten so "good" at being recovering alcoholics that they forget what it's like to actually "need" a meeting no matter what.

SARA B.
Hawkesbury, Ontario

CHAPTER 5

TO LOVE AND BE LOVED

Members reach out for help—and to help others—when heartache and loneliness threaten to shatter their sobriety

Divorced or single, AAs dwelling on heartache find that the solution is turning to others who are also hurting. "It's hard for me to be alone, wanting someone to love, and to be loved in return, wondering if God has forgotten me," a member writes. "However, God's time is not my time, as well you know." In these stories, the pain of loneliness is eased by working with another alcoholic. "The answer for my pain was in the Twelfth Step," one single member writes. "If I am in pain, it may be beneficial to me if I am aware of those in even more pain."

Self-Support JULY 2007

It was just another run-of-the-mill night at Harvard Street, except I'd arrived at the meeting to find one of my sober sisters in deep distress. When I went to hug her and asked what was wrong, she told me that her marriage was in serious trouble. On top of that, her finances were in catastrophic shape and her business was collapsing. My friend's sobs as the meeting began were audible.

Hearing them, my mind traveled back, and I realized it was exactly two years ago that night that I had walked into this, my home group, in much the same state. Married at the time, I had just caught my partner of seven years, who had lost his sobriety and had been struggling to get it back, in a devastating set of lies and betrayals. I had realized that, for the sake of my own sobriety, our marriage could not continue. Packing an overnight bag, I came straight to the meeting. Once there, I fell into a heap at my sponsor's feet and wept like I was being cut in pieces.

Until that moment I had done a tremendous amount of service in AA. At any given time, I had several commitments, sponsored women, spoke frequently about my marvelous life in sobriety, and worked with multiple newcomers. I believed, as the Big Book says, that it was crucial to extend help to other AAs if I wanted to stay sober myself. As for receiving it, well, with a little bit of time under my belt, that was better left to those who needed it more.

But that night, and in the weeks and months that followed, everything changed. I slowly and completely went to pieces. Not only had I lost my marriage, but my home, most of my possessions, and my ability to work at my chosen profession. To top it all off, my husband had left me with a mountain of credit card debt. I had a shattered heart, no career prospects, and a sense of despair and betrayal so pervasive I was positive it would engulf me completely.

Absolutely crippled by my losses, I struggled just to show up. Gone was the cheery face gleaming at every newcomer. Gone was the certainty that God would care for me, you, or any one of us. Gone was the wherewithal to do any service for AA but the most rudimentary. I felt like a ghost.

My sponsor and sober girlfriends, thank God, proceeded to support me at every turn. I was like a sick child passed from arm to arm. Never once was I set down. Many was the time I sat sobbing at Harvard Street or some other meeting, thinking, I can't share about my divorce again. They're all sick of me! And then some kind face would nod at me across the room, or some soft elbow nudge, and I would put up my hand. Again. And grieve to the room. Again. I tried desperately to make my shares "recovery-related," but even when I couldn't I was told it was OK, that it was recovery enough just seeing me stay sober through my troubles.

After the meeting, I was invariably surrounded. Never once was I told I was "too much." It seemed there was enough support to carry even my world of pain. I continued to come. I did a Step workshop with some close girlfriends. I kept sponsoring, even if it was fewer women, and even though I felt much less of an "inspiration" than before. I stayed close, and took life a second at a time.

Very slowly, so slowly I barely discerned it was happening, I began to feel better. I began to get better. I can still remember the first night I went to Harvard Street and did not cry. A milestone! And the day I got my first promotion at work. Or when I announced, to cheers, that my divorce had finally gone through. Only a couple of weeks ago I informed the room, with tears in my eyes, that I had paid off the last of my debt. What a surge of congratulations that set off! Along the way, it once again became normal for me to be OK on Monday nights. I found myself even smiling on occasion.

The topic for tonight's meeting was the Seventh Tradition. Our speaker set a tone that inspired deep and heartfelt shares. Then my sober sister shared, pouring her heart out about her troubles. We listened, silently.

Then, without thinking, I raised my hand. I said that although there are many times when we "alks" need to be self-supporting, I had learned that there were times that I needed to let go of my desperate desire to do it myself and allow support from others. The wisdom was in knowing when one was appropriate and when the other was not. Surrendering to my alcoholism was an example of something I ought not try alone. Getting through calamities was another. Developing a sense of self-esteem, however, I found was an inside job. And it didn't hurt to know how to pay my own bills, either.

I spoke of the recent months and years, and how without AA's support first, self-support could never have become possible for me. However, tonight I could honestly say I was doing OK. I was out of debt, financially stable, living in a sweet little home, starting a new career, single, and happy. In fact, I could see that, as devastatingly difficult as they had been, the last two years had been a giant Seventh Tradition workshop. Never in my married life or at any time before it had I truly understood what being self-supporting meant. I had relied on others to take care of me, not just financially, but emotionally and spiritually, too, and I let my life go to hell if they didn't.

Because of what I'd gone through I can now see that when I truly let go of old and self-destructive habits and relationships (or have them torn from me), God replaces them with a healthy supply of support—provided I make some contributions (take some actions).

I closed my share by repeating that the beauty of sobriety is that sometimes I am the one supported, and other times the one supporting. One act helps destroy my ego, the other my self-centeredness. I need to practice both actions if I want to survive.

The meeting ended. I found my sober sister. She said she'd like to talk. For the next half-hour I listened while she poured out her pain and consternation. I didn't tell her what to do. I couldn't; I had no idea. I told her only what I had been told two years ago: that, whatever happened, divorce or no divorce, bankruptcy or not, if she didn't drink she would get through it. Or, rather, we would. Together. I was living proof of this.

My friend nodded sadly, and with just the faintest glimmer of hope. Once again, I felt the truth of the Promise: "No matter how far down the scale we have gone we will see how our experience can benefit others."

JESSICA C.
Los Angeles, California

Life, Not Regrets JULY 2007
(From Dear Grapevine)

Today I celebrate eighteen months without a drink.

I'm also divorced two years from a thirty-plus year marriage. One day, after sitting alone, soaked in tears and feeling empty, worthless, and crippled in the smallest task, I reached out and gave my phone number to someone else—they were hurting, too. In that simplest of acts, my world changed.

I thank AA for helping me live my life instead of my regrets.

VALERIE
Salt Lake City, Utah

Love and Death—
One Day at a Time FEBRUARY 2003

When I was about a year sober, I met and fell in love with a wonderful man. It was an awesome experience. I started concentrating more on the Steps and living life on life's terms. I called my sponsor more and went to more meetings than I had when I first came into AA. I realized I had no idea how to have a healthy relationship. My sponsor told me that learning more about myself through the Steps would help me in my relationships with others.

Unfortunately, the wonderful man I had fallen in love with had cancer. I watched him go through so much because of that deadly disease—chemotherapy, radiation, several hospital stays, and surgery. His future was very uncertain, yet I saw this beautiful human being enjoy life—he laughed, he smiled a genuine smile, and he was kind and loving toward everyone. I received many blessings from this relationship, but the most profound gift he gave me was showing me how to live one day at a time.

We had dated for only eighteen months before he died at his parents' home in Fort Wayne, Indiana. I spent much of my time there praying for acceptance and peace—for Tom as well as for myself. Ultimately, the day came when I accepted my powerlessness over his fate. That was the day God gave me the honor of being there when Tom took his last breath. I have been changed forever by the impression this man made on my life. He was part of the gift of this beautiful program, and I don't want to ever take any of it for granted.

JEAN B.
Franklin, Indiana

Riding It Out JULY 1997

I almost drank last week. Summer was over and September found me living in New York City, over nine years sober, nearing forty, newly single and freshly laid-off. For fifteen months I'd been experiencing a painful stretch of recovery. I had watched other alcoholics struggle through similar patches. It's a difficult shedding of skin, a remaking for long-term sobriety. I also think it's one reason why we see such a dropping off of attendance at meetings around year seven or eight.

Thankfully, in the previous year or more of turmoil I'd stayed close to meetings as well as to my Higher Power, my sponsor, and good friends in the rooms of AA. Only rarely did I lose the belief that all that was happening was because of sobriety, not in spite of it.

It had gotten rough around my eighth anniversary. I had begun to use the Steps to understand why my work life in the theater, never very lucrative, had also become so unsatisfying. Keeping the slogan "awareness, acceptance, action," in mind, I was seeing progress, though certainly not perfection. Yet I felt confident. A year or so of attention to this, I thought, and my Higher Power and I will have me happily working somewhere and bringing home some real money to boot.

I shouldn't have spoken for my Higher Power, who had other plans. A serious health scare left my wife and I with unwelcome thoughts of mortality and how each of us wanted to live the second half of our lives. During our time together, we'd gotten drunk, bottomed out, and found AA. In our years in the Fellowship we had jointly started two meetings, which are both doing beautifully today. Now, with many tears, we saw that we were no longer helping each others' recovery and needed to end our married life together. We managed to do so gently and lovingly. Talk about miracles of sobriety.

By spring, just in time for my ninth anniversary, I was living alone for the first time since the lost years of my early twenties. It was hard to believe that I wouldn't fall back into the spirit-breaking isolation and loneliness of that time. Back then my first thought of the morning was a curse: "Oh ----, I'm awake. How many hours until I can sleep again?" A new year or a birthday seared me with the truth of another empty year passing.

Of course now I had nine years of sober reference, and a program for living. I wanted to believe that that would make the difference. My mantra was "Establish good habits," and I tried to live by it. I brought good food into the house and prepared and ate it. I can't tell you how much that surprised and pleased me, and gave me hope. I made plans with people. I didn't wait for them to call me; I called them. This was hard since isolation has been one of the slowest areas of recovery for me. I don't really believe that I have much to offer anyone beyond my professional skills; I can be a blast in a rehearsal hall, but I'm kind of stiff at a party. So it wasn't easy, but I organized outings, and I joined the group for coffee or dinner after meetings.

I did other scary things too. As I explained to a very patient woman in a candlelit Greenwich Village coffeehouse, I hadn't been out on a first date for many years.

Things were going well but I felt a great need to get on with my life, to make big changes, find a new career. I cooked up some grandiose plans but whenever I took action to implement them, a quiet voice in my head said, "Slow down. You want to know what to do? Take the summer off. Stay in Brooklyn. Ride your bike. Eat salads. Write." I listened.

By Labor Day I felt strong again, physically, mentally, and spiritually. I accepted the bad news that the job I expected to return to no longer existed. It felt like a bottom and I welcomed it. It was easy to say to my Higher Power, "Your will, not mine be done," because I had no idea myself of what to do. With faith and some savings I was willing to wait until more was revealed.

During the following two weeks I went to my meetings, talked to people, took a few job actions offered up by my Higher Power, and prepared for a Fourth Step on my work history. I also made calls trying to find someone to join me for a big New York City bicycling event the upcoming Sunday, when thousands of bikers would be covering one hundred miles in the five boroughs.

That Sunday I set off with Steve, a new nonalcoholic friend who didn't know I was in AA. It was a beautiful day, clear, in the low eighties, perfect for cycling. The sunshine was just beginning to take on fall's golden hue. The good weather was a surprise; rain had been expected. It felt great to be sober.

Steve was the perfect guy to traverse New York with. He works for one of the preservation boards and really knows city history. We passed elegant houses high on a Brooklyn hill, circled a reservoir, saw the remnants of the 1964 World's Fair and, in the distance, Shea Stadium. We ate Indian food in Jackson Heights, then we headed for the Queens warehouse district on the East River and the last leg of our ride. I was in the midst of a glorious day, so different from my worst fears of life after divorce. I was grateful for this gift of sobriety. A drink was the last thing on my mind.

Heading west, we could see that suddenly serious weather was gathering over the Manhattan skyline. The temperature started dropping fast, and as we crossed under the Williamsburg Bridge it was certain that we were in for a drenching any minute. A good rainstorm is one of my favorite things, but just a few blocks further on the air turned nearly dark as night, with a sickly greenish-yellow tint to what little light there was. And when the clouds opened up, it was ice that fell, not rain.

It was clear that we were going to have to hole up and fast. But where? This industrial neighborhood appeared deserted on this weekend afternoon. Then, there on our left: a bar. And leaning out of the doors: four young women, beckoning and calling for us to come in. Believe it or not, what passed through my mind was the thought of the Sirens of Greek mythology, women whose beautiful song drew sailors to their death on the shoals—passed through and then out. In a few seconds Steve and I and our bicycles were inside. Beyond the windows, it stormed.

It was an artists' bar, serving the creative urban pioneers drawn to the area by its cheap rents and ample space to paint or sculpt. I love artists' bars; I had worked in one for years when I was active. I love the women in artists' bars; I had married one.

Now, I've been in drinking situations before, usually without any problem. In those instances I had, as our literature suggests, good reason to be there. I thought it through before I went, did a check of my motives and an inventory of my sobriety. If anything seemed amiss, I didn't go! If I started to feel uncomfortable I got out!

This time around, there had been no preparation. It was just me, elated from the exercise, and the storm and the women. That was all my disease, dormant for many years, needed.

I ordered a bottled water from the bartender, but he had his hands full and there was a delay. While I waited, a pretty young woman with an exotic accent sat next to me, ordered a beer, and gave me a lovely smile.

And here it came. Instantly my thinking took on the kind of illogic that I could sustain for years when I was active. I thought: My Higher Power has delivered me to this wonderful moment. It is a transcendent event. A drink now would not interrupt my sobriety because this is a time apart. I should, I must, have a drink.

In my years sober I've had occasional drink signals, watching a beer commercial or seeing cognac served at a restaurant. I believe that it is because I go to meetings regularly that the urge is immediately followed by the saving thought: Remember who you are. That Sunday no such thought occurred. All that came up was a vague unease about my reasoning. It was effortlessly ignored. My designer water was still undelivered. I was looking at the top-shelf bourbon and feeling the storm's chill on my damp skin.

Thanks only to the Higher Power that I try to contact every day in meetings and in prayer, I finally began to listen to the tentative question in my head: Are you sure that a drink now won't cost you your sobriety?

Yes, I'm sure. This is beyond sobriety.

Please think for a moment.

I did. The doubt grew stronger. The desire to drink passed.

The storm also passed, and we left the bar, and I was soon home. I talked to my sponsor that night but not until I related the story at a beginners' meeting the next day did I fully experience what had happened. Sitting there after speaking I realized that, had I drunk, the best-case scenario would see me at that meeting announcing my one day back. I felt something of how devastating that would have been. Of course there was no guarantee I would have even made it to that meeting.

A few days later I heard someone share with a single day back after eleven years of sobriety. He had fallen away from the Fellowship, showing up at a single meeting a year to mark his anniversary. Finally he slipped. In despair, he spoke with great eloquence of what he had lost. It was exactly as I imagined it to be. I gave him my phone number and asked him to call me.

JOSH B.
Brooklyn, New York

Adult Love JANUARY 2004

(Excerpt)

I am a thirty-eight year old AA member. I will soon be divorced, after seventeen years of what I thought was an okay marriage. It had its ups and downs, mostly down while I was actively drinking and heading for the bottom. My wife stood by me through all of that, until after I had admitted defeat and had somehow, with the helping hand of AA and my sponsor, not to mention an incredible treatment facility, acquired nearly three years of sobriety, one day at a time.

Three years into that sobriety, my wife decided she no longer knew the man she married and could not forgive and forget, in spite of my growth and involvement with the program. I, of course, thought everything was getting better, and was completely emotionally blindsided. I didn't have any idea she was so unhappy. It was not too little, but it was too late.

Imagine my surprise when I did not take that first drink! It was my first realization that my Higher Power had removed my obsession, and that I truly was in this program for me. I am grateful for each new day, even during these very difficult times, and for the many who supported me. I am active in my home group and attend many meetings in my area as well. It staves off the loneliness of being on my own.

It's hard for me to be alone, wanting someone to love, and to be loved in return, wondering if God has forgotten me. However, God's time is not my time, as well you know, and patience comes so hard to all of us. There are many of us lost souls in the program, suffering this way.

I can only believe that if the Higher Power believes I am not ready for someone in my life, I must accept that, for I am not God. As painful as it is for me to do so, I can only admit that, at this point in my sobriety, I would only repeat my needy adolescent behavior in any new relationship, and would hurt other innocent people in and out of the program. In the previously cited article, Bill W. concurs: "Those adolescent urges that so many of us have for top approval, perfect security and perfect romance—urges quite appropriate to the age of seventeen—prove to be an impossible way of life when we are at age forty-seven or fifty-seven," and I might add, thirty-one or thirty-eight.

Of course, none of this seems to help when the evening draws near, and I am alone in unfamiliar surroundings. My faith seems to flee before my fears. I selfishly want what I want, desire relief in the comfort of someone's, anyone's, arms. But twenty-four hours is all

I have to bear. One day leads to the next, no matter how unhappy I choose to be. My Higher Power has never given me more than I could bear in one day.

TROY C.
Sioux Rapids, Iowa

In the Center of Sorrow

FEBRUARY 2007

Two weeks before Christmas at my home group, I raised my hand and said that I was celebrating seventeen years without a drink. I gave credit to my Higher Power, the group, my sponsor, the program, meetings, and my willingness to put in the work. Each part was important in making it happen, I said.

That evening, my other half and I went to a holiday gathering. We sat in front of a warm fireplace and shared fellowship with friends. It was a perfect ending to the day. I went to sleep sober with a smile on my face and a grateful heart.

After saving for many years, we had bought our dream home and had an appointment to sign the final papers in two days. Uprooting our lives and packing for the move had been stressful, but still, things couldn't get much better.

Unfortunately, they got worse, much worse.

When I woke up the next morning, I took my usual few minutes to think about the day ahead. It was our last day in the old house, and there was last-minute packing to finish. I passed through the living room on my way to the kitchen to make coffee and saw my partner asleep in his chair—not an uncommon sight.

When I tried to wake him, I realized he wasn't breathing. I called 9-1-1, started cardiopulmonary resuscitation, and wanted to get drunk more than I ever had during my seventeen years of sobriety.

This couldn't be happening, I thought. Deny it, it's not happening. Drunk. Get drunk. This isn't fair.

My heart ripped into pieces. I continued CPR as the 9-1-1 operator talked me through the procedure. The paramedics arrived, and within moments the three of them were working on him like a six-handed lifesaving machine. Instead of looking for a bottle, I called a friend from my home group, told him what had happened, and asked him to meet me at the hospital. I was a mess and unable to drive; a deputy sheriff took me to the hospital.

My friend sat with me in the waiting area. When the nurse came, I saw in her eyes that the news was not good. They couldn't save him. My world crashed.

If the desire to be drunk had been strong before, it was nothing compared to what followed. Thankfully, I was not alone. My friend offered all the support he could as we started paperwork, made phone calls, and contacted my partner's out-of-town family. More program friends met us at my house. The phone rang and the doorbell chimed constantly in endless songs of support. A neighbor, also a sober member of AA, and his wife brought plates of food to feed the growing crowd. There was nothing anyone could do to make it better for me, but they kept me from picking up a drink and making it worse.

I was beyond consolation and in a fog the first few days, unable to see past the pain. My AA friends told me when to eat, when to sleep, and when to go to a meeting. They reluctantly respected my wish to be alone for a few hours at night when I tried to sleep.

As long as I do my part, I know I will get through this, even though I want to stay home to grieve and cry. I want to isolate and not show anyone my "weaker" side. But I go to my regular meetings, even if I don't want to. Each day, I call at least three people in Alcoholics Anonymous, even if I don't want to. It hurts, but I practice the Steps around my grief, fear, guilt, and loneliness, even though I don't want to. I relive the pain and write it down, even though I don't want to.

When I went to my first AA meeting more than seventeen years ago, members said I didn't have to drink, even if I wanted to. Now, to keep my part of the bargain, I do what the program has taught me to do, even if I don't want to.

I came into AA alone. Even with a handful of drinking buddies, I was still alone. Seventeen years later, with less than twenty-four hours' notice by word-of-mouth, more than 200 sober members of AA came to the memorial visitation for my partner. The Fellowship made a big impression on his family. The message that AA carried showed how much he was loved and respected, and it was a priceless gift. Two weeks after the service, his mother called and asked for the address of the "friend of Bill" whom everyone talked about. The group's show of support touched his family and gave them more comfort than words ever could.

When my partner and I first moved to this area many years ago, we were the first open same-sex couple at local meetings. We learned later that some people wouldn't come to meetings that he and I attended. We showed up anyway, because as recovering alcoholics, meetings were a vital part of our sobriety. Ironically, some who had shunned us gave me the most support after his death.

I still have a huge gaping hole in my heart because my partner meant the world to me. I don't know how I can go on without him. But I keep putting one foot in front of the other, one day at a time. My experiences in most areas of my life have shown me that if I show up and do what's in front of me, I will be fine. I haven't had a problem yet that practicing the principles, Traditions, and Steps hasn't helped solve. I suspect that will hold true with my grief, fear, and loneliness, too. I just have to keep doing what I should, even if I don't want to.

MARK H.
Bartlett, Illinois

Gruff Love OCTOBER 2006

At a recent meeting, we discussed the Twelfth Step. The leader spoke, in part, about the unfairness of life and a God who allows injustice to take place. His sibling had died some months ago and he still struggled to come to terms with his loss.

I left the meeting disappointed with myself for having offered sympathy without drawing on my own experience. His lingering grief reminded me of a time, thirteen years earlier, when I had shared from a similar painful place. I hadn't shared about a death, although I too had lost siblings in recovery. I shared about the pain I felt from a then-recent marital separation.

Back then, when I finished, a man raised his hand. I remember little of his share, except roughly these words, and the impatient tone with which they were said: "Go find a newcomer to work with."

What an unfeeling, unkind, SOB he was for offering such a facile solution, I remember thinking. In fact, I worked with a newcomer at the time who called me frequently, but his calls seemed like a small bandage on my gaping wound.

Hundreds of people have been kind to me in recovery since then and for the most part, I have no memory of their kindness. However, this man and his gruff words remain in my mind. I remember him as a man without much in the way of material assets, someone who lived alone and knew the pain of loneliness. He looked like a man who had his ups and downs, who was older—at an age where things like money and love were unlikely to come.

I remember his words because he spoke not from politeness or easily dispensed solicitude, but from the truth of his own experience. He told me what all great spiritual teachers knew and continue to know, that the world can be a place of suffering and pain as well as joy, and that it's not about fairness and getting my needs met and all the rest. If it were about fairness, I might not have the gift of sobriety, given my flawed character and outrageous behavior when I drank.

If I am in pain, this man was saying, it may be beneficial to me if I am aware of those in even more pain. He tried to remind me that the answer for my pain was in the Twelfth Step, and in the spiritual conditioning required to live in the fulfillment of it.

DAVID S.
New York, New York

PART THREE
FINANCIAL ADVERSITY

CHAPTER 6
PAYCHECK TO PAYCHECK, MEETING TO MEETING

Unemployed AAs hold on to hope and the Fellowship
one day at a time

After being laid off, these AAs go to more meetings, make more phone calls to fellow AAs, explore new career directions ... and try to trust in their Higher Power. As they adjust to a difficult situation and try to figure out their next moves, not all of them simply sit back and accept their fate. One comes up with a strategy with his sponsor to make an appeal to get his job back. Another needs several people, including his sponsor, to talk him out of getting even with the boss who laid him off. And some find good results when they let go and let God. Having no luck finding work in her own field, one AA finds unexpected work, which she loves, in a brand new field. "All my preconceived notions of what should be shut out the possibility of a Higher Power's intervention," she writes.

Fired Up! SEPTEMBER 2010

My young sponsee, sober for six months, was unfairly laid off. He felt blindsided by his employer and, though he tried to remain stoic about this tragedy, you could tell that inwardly his world was beginning to unravel. Living from paycheck to paycheck like most Americans, being fired and left penniless, he was now unable to pay rent or take care of the barest necessities.

The young man had been faithfully paying off debts, but now saw himself sinking into deep despair because of this enormous burden. He was one step away from becoming homeless. The only effective solution I could offer him was Chapter 10, "To Employers" in the Big Book, which has a well-reasoned guide for newcomers learning how to do well on the job, and ways sponsors can assist the recovering worker to function better.

I encouraged the young man to go see the CEO of the corporation where he worked, wearing his best suit and armed with five "talking points" to present his case: 1) He was a great worker who delivered 100%, 2) He worked well with staff and clients, 3) He had used his personal and vacation time to deal with any medical issues, 4) He firmly believed this was a misunderstanding and not a major infraction, and 5) Most importantly, as a recovering alcoholic he believed he had become the rock-solid employee the company expected.

The CEO listened very intently and asked his aide if the young man was a good worker. The reply was, "Yes, no one has ever complained, only complimented him on his good service." "Fine," the CEO responded. "Let me make a few inquiries, and I'll get back with you shortly." I picked my sponsee up after his meeting and we went to a restaurant where we did a quick inventory of the day's events, continued to pray for and meditate on all of the day's par-

ticipants, and filled out and sent thank you cards to the human resources manager, the CEO and the others involved.

I received a call from my sponsee about 90 minutes later with
wonderful news. He had been reinstated, and would start work after bringing a required note from his doctor. He said that all wasn't
perfect with work, but he now had a Big Book Chapter 10 format
to resolve similar problems, and wanted to use the literature to en-
hance his social, financial and spiritual recovery as well.

As a sponsor I am always comforted when I can utilize our AA
literature to aid the person who still suffers and help him find and
pick up that spiritual kit of tools laid at our feet.

JOSE G.
Port Orchard, Wash.

Out of Work, But Not Hope

DECEMBER 2000 *(From Dear Grapevine)*

I wish to share my feelings on the saying, "If you just don't pick up
the first drink, everything will be okay." Like a lot of recovering alcoholics, I chafed at that idea in early sobriety because in some ways
my life seemed to get worse. One year into sobriety, I was downsized
from my job in a bad economy. I went to meetings, kept in touch with
my sponsor, and, above all, didn't pick up that first drink.

Since then, employment has been a catch-as-catch-can situation
for someone who while drinking held a long-term, well-paid position. Despite the financial and employment ups and downs to the
present day, twelve years after the original layoff, I'm grateful for that
saying. Many times I wondered if my life would ever feel stable again.
Then I'd realize that I had a lot to be grateful for due to being sober.

As I continue to struggle, I think of the words of an old-timer
in my area. No matter what the topic, he always finishes sharing

with the words, "and I haven't had a drink today." Remembering his words never fails to bring to my mind the words "experience, strength, and hope."

ANONYMOUS

Through the Darkest Days

MAY 2005

When I was five years sober, I was twenty-three years old and I had just been laid off from a seasonal job. I had a new wife, new child, and had put a college education on hold in order to take care of my family. I was learning to deal with life on life's terms. I was attending meetings regularly, had a home group, and was in service there. My career goals were slipping away and I was struggling to raise a family and pay bills, and hoped to improve from the financial situation I was in. Out of desperation, I shared a thought I believed was insanity with my recovering wife. I had told her I was thinking about the military as a solution—that I could have a steady paycheck, get some money for college, and get out in a few years. She thought it was a reasonable idea.

I did not check with anyone in my group or with my sponsor, because I sensed I was being foolish and they would stop me. Nobody in my home group had ever joined the military before. I saw a recruiter from each of the services, and then I went to my home group and I reluctantly shared my recent experiences and what I thought was the solution. We had a podium that seemed to bring the truth out of people when they began sharing.

After the meeting I was told that it was a sane thought, and that I had been sober and active in AA long enough to be able to make such life decisions. My sponsor recommended I take an inventory of the situation and I did. It turned out that the second person I asked to listen to my inventory was the child of a military officer who had grown up in the lifestyle I was considering.

I joined the Army in February 1989 with five years of sobriety. I cried when I said goodbye to my home group. During basic training, I used the chapel as a means of spiritual guidance because meetings were not available. Once I arrived at my first duty station, I followed the directions of those who had been sober and traveled or sober and incarcerated—I found a meeting. I was told that it is critical to find a meeting of Alcoholics Anonymous as soon as possible, and preferably within the first twenty-four hours of arriving at a new location or leaving an institution. This is important for me because the thought often creeps in "nobody knows me here."

I called AA before the furniture arrived. I made contact and found there were meetings on base. I have since learned that most military installations have at least one meeting on post and usually several nearby. I had lots of preconceived notions about sober life in the Army, which eventually were replaced with the truth as I gained experience, strength, and hope. I did not think it appropriate to go to meetings in uniform, since AA is a place where there are no leaders and there ought to be no rank. Well, when that is the suit you wear all day, it is difficult to change and it is especially impractical to change in the middle of the duty day. I learned that we are all equal inside the rooms, anyway. I learned to call people "Mike" in the meeting and "Sir" once we left.

I enjoyed success in the Army, and looking back, I believe it is mostly because I was sober and mature enough to be ready to be a good employee. I had a desire to serve and was put into the personnel administration field.

I had no idea what I wanted to be when I grew up, so I thought the recruiters would give me a test and tell me what I should be. I had rationalized that if they told me I should be a firefighter, it would be God's will and the pressure for me to make a decision would be off. Instead, they told me I tested very well and was qualified for any job they had. They handed me a list of jobs to choose from.

All I knew from AA was that I wanted to be of service to God and my fellows. They suggested I be the Chaplain's Assistant. I would have taken it but my misunderstanding of career progression in the military led me to assume that you would someday be promoted to Chaplain, and I didn't think that was for me. Today, our Chaplain's Assistant takes care of the collection, makes coffee after our service, and sets up chairs for our socials. Who knew that these were skills I had already honed back in my original home group?

The office job I had envisioned was not accurate either. I spent over half of my first two years in the field with an airborne unit. It was a new and exciting experience to jump out of airplanes. I used the Third Step prayer every single time I jumped and still do to this day. In 1990, we were notified we were deploying to the Middle East. I was afraid; I had drifted away from AA, finding my new group did not feel as comfortable as my first home group. I prayed and wrote a letter to the General Service Office asking them to forward a Grapevine and to pray for us. What I got was an incredible experience!

I truly was worried about staying sober, even in a country that was reputed to have no alcohol. Upon arriving, we were very busy. Much of our equipment was still green and had to be painted or exchanged for desert camouflage stuff. We lived in tents at first until a contracting officer could find us a better home. We later moved to an old horse stable, but the cinderblock buildings were a great improvement until the ground war began.

I put a notice on the bulletin board that said, "Friends of Bill W. meet here every night at 1900 hours." I waited with a Big Book in my hand, which I thought was easy to recognize for anyone familiar with AA. Nobody ever came. I relied on my literature and a few tapes through the next few months. Once, when I was so lonely and desperate the thought of a drink came into my mind and I began to feel the desire to drink. I considered the choices, considering the black market supply I knew had come from Bahrain, or the near-beer they served in our recreation tent. I began to be consumed by the mental obsession, even after seven years without a drink! I cried myself to sleep that night and postponed the drink for just one more day. "One day at a Time" truly saved my life, because the next day did not seem so bad. The Scud alerts were becoming more frequent and fear was a real part of my life. Even though these weapons did not turn out to be extremely devastating, the fear at that moment was very real. I took the Big Book and a picture of my family to the bunker every time there was an alarm.

About this time, the miracle began to occur, just when I needed it the most. I began to receive my first pieces of mail from members of AA who got my address from the Loners/Internationalists program at GSO. This is what our General Service Office did for me when I wrote and asked for help. They placed my name and address along with other service members on a list and circulated it among trusted servants in the Fellowship. The result was that when I put off that drink for one more day, I began to get the love of our Fellowship delivered in a mail pouch. At first it was a few letters and a card from an AA group. This was enough to give me hope. As the days went on the amount of mail increased. I was now getting cards, letters, speaker tapes, literature, and even a care package with goodies in it. I often got five to ten pieces of mail in a day, although the delivery was sporadic and we usually only received mail three times a week. At the peak of this postal miracle, I got thirty-six pieces of mail from AA members all over the country. My fellow soldiers did not know why I was getting so much mail; I told them I had a fan club. Actually I did; I had a host of friends who loved me through one of the darkest times in my recovery, even though they had never laid eyes on me in their lives. We still shared a common bond and they were able to send the hand of AA halfway around the world to be there.

I returned home safe and sound, as most of us did during that war. I continued on in my military career and still serve after sixteen years. So much for getting the college money and moving on.

I have found that the military is a great place to serve Alcoholics Anonymous. I am successful in my profession and have been blessed to pass my experience, strength, and hope on to many uniformed and civilian alcoholics. During each deployment I have been familiar with since my own experience, I seek to repay those who helped me by sending letters and literature and seeking out those who might be trying to not drink a day at a time.

Today there are many military members serving in harm's way who have battled with alcoholism and been defeated. Alcoholics Anonymous has worked to help us meet calamity with serenity in a variety of circumstances. Since World War II, members of AA have used literature to help carry the message of hope to our service men and women in recovery. From my own experiences and many observations, they will return transformed in some way.

ROGER W.
Shape, Belgium

Eyeliner, Anyone? JULY 2004

"The grouch and the brainstorm were not for us"
—Alcoholics Anonymous

During my first nine years of sobriety, I had learned that the grouches I liked to display didn't get me what I wanted or needed, and I did not give in to this old behavior frequently. But the brainstorm? I valued my brainstorms and believed that that part of the Big Book surely wasn't meant for me. How much I still had to learn.

In my ninth year of sobriety, I was fired as part of a staff reduction at work because of the sagging economy in our area. I was devastated. Anger always comes first with me, masking the feelings of rejection, abandonment, self-pity, and last, but never least—pride.

The people in AA were compassionate and supportive. I was given many suggestions, some based on experience, some on other peoples' brainstorms. I followed through on the more practical suggestions, applying for unemployment, submitting applications to places that could use my skills, opening my mind to a new career path, and talking it over with my Higher Power to ask for his help.

But after I had taken all of the actions, I found it hard to sit and wait. I always had been an action-oriented person and took pride in tackling problems head-on. "Don't just sit there, do something" was my war cry. Unfortunately, I mistook frantic activity—based on brainstorms—for well-thought-out action. I thought my brainstorms were God-inspired solutions.

Webster's dictionary says a brainstorm is "a violent transient mental derangement"—in other words, "a harebrained idea."

I had to do something and when I heard about someone else's brainstorm, I took it for my own. I invested my retirement funds in a party-plan cosmetics dealership. When I filled out a questionnaire to see if I was fitted for this line of work, I failed it miserably. But the people at headquarters must have been on break when my form came in, because they quickly cashed my check, sent me twenty boxes of cosmetics, and wished me great luck.

After I'd sold cosmetics to my reluctant friends and family, my little business died. I just did not have what it took to be successful in such an endeavor. The questionnaire knew it; now I knew it.

Looking back, I see I was like a person sitting in a train depot, clutching a ticket, waiting for her scheduled train. But waiting is difficult, so I jumped on the first train that started to move, not knowing what city it was going to or even if it was going in the right direction.

When I first became unemployed, I took the necessary actions and turned the outcome over to the Higher Power. I should have waited for God to do his work. Instead, I went with the first brainstorm that came along. In God's time, I was hired back by my former employer in a different position, which I liked far better than my old one.

The lessons learned were expensive in terms of time, money, and serenity, but I did learn to wait for the right train. By the way, does anyone want to buy some eyeliner?

N.H.
Sterling, Illinois

The Phone Fix DECEMBER 2001

There was an AA meeting in Westbrook, Connecticut, where I saw a sign that said: "Pick Up the Phone Before You Pick Up a Drink." The people at that meeting told me to get a sponsor, make phone calls, and do some caring and sharing, and I would feel better and my life would improve.

I was thirty-eight years old, divorced, raising my teenage son alone, unemployed and unemployable, reactive, withdrawn, and complaining. I wondered: did I have much to lose by being teachable? By not changing much in my life, just everything?

So I started making phone calls to people when I was angry, frustrated, lonely, scared, confused—and also when I was happy, excited, inspired, fulfilled. Gradually I started to listen. I began getting to know everyone in my AA community on a first-name basis. That was incredibly affirming. At every turn there was a "Hi, Margo." One time I was very down and a chap who was much less well-off than I said "Hi, Margo" when he saw me on the street. It turned my day completely around!

I rented out rooms on the first floor of my house. The tenants told me, "The phone never rings in this house." That was because I was going from call to call. When I had an incoming call and was on the other line, I would see who it was and then call them back after completing the current call. That was an extreme time when I was going through a lot of stress. The support was incredible.

One person who had a tiny room, a mattress on the floor, and a phone coaxed me out of a depression into a committed relationship. We were matrons of honor for each other at our weddings, two weeks apart, in 1989.

Today, after sixteen years of sobriety, I am employed and I have good relationships with my family—happy, joyous, free, inspired, and fulfilled. I have two sponsors whom I call sporadically, a family with whom I check in by phone once a week, and a lot of pals with whom I can share where I am and what I'm feeling. Just as I abused alcohol and drugs on good days, bad days, sunny days, rainy days, I call friends or family on those occasions. When I get "ten-ton telephonitis" and can't pick up the phone, I know that I am in trouble.

MARGO A.
Washington, D.C.

Dependence on His Higher Power Led Him to a Greater Sense of Independence

OCTOBER 1979

I had been sitting around AA tables for over three years, dutifully reciting how I had turned my life and will over to the care of God, when a crisis entered my life.

On a cold December day, shortly before Christmas, I found myself out of a job—fired because I had entered into a personal conflict with my boss.

My first reaction, typical of most alcoholics', was to get even in some way. I called upon an AA friend, who led me to a lawyer, also in AA, who calmly listened to my tale of woe and then suggested I forget the whole thing and start anew that day.

Not content with the lawyer's simple suggestion, I boarded the commuter train and, for the next thirty minutes, rode along engrossed in "self-will run riot" plots of ways to get even for the wrong that had been done to me.

Knowing full well that I was in a precarious position, I surrounded myself with AA friends and meetings for the next two weeks. However, the fate that had befallen me would not go away. I wanted to get even.

About two weeks into my mad-dog approach to my job loss, I went to an AA breakfast and talked to a doctor friend of mine. He listened to my story and then calmly said, "Bill, if you have really turned your life and will over to the care of God, as you've been saying at meetings, then you will accept your situation as God's will for you."

It sounded so simple, I really couldn't believe my ears.

That was it. I had been sitting around AA meetings, parroting the Third Step, but I really hadn't done it at all.

I called my sponsor, and we sat down to talk over coffee. Much to my amazement, my sponsor echoed the same words I had heard earlier from my doctor friend in AA. "Not only will you accept this as God's will for you, but you will, in due time, find out it was the best thing for you," he said. Since that time, I have faced many a crisis with the same outlook—realizing God knows what is best for me.

By simply placing my dependence (with no reservations) on God's will for me, I actually became more independent.

Today, I am grateful for the AA program and for the simple knowledge of each of the Twelve Steps of the program.

W. C.
Chicago, Illinois

Lifetime Dream MARCH 2010

The baseline of what I need to survive is different from most, as I am a Gulf War veteran. I lived in the desert for six months without any creature comforts. I can remember sitting in a structurally unsound bunker with 53 others, packed in like sardines. You could smell the fear. Someone suggested we all say what wc would do if wc ever got out of the bunker. I said I would ride horses in Ireland. The laughter at the thought popped the tension balloon. Soon we learned that this was only a drill, and I forgot about this desire.

It's now 17 years later. I've been sober for 10 years. Thanks to hard work, careful planning and a prestigious job that paid well, I was able to live the dream of a lifetime: a trip to Ireland, where I got to ride a horse!

While atop my horse, a new friend asked, "While you were in the war, did you ever think you would be riding horses in Ireland?" For a few seconds I was back in that bunker. I could smell the sweat and fear, and remember the laughter. I saw how all the laughter and tears had led to this moment, and life just made sense. "As a matter of fact, I have," I replied. No one else seemed to notice the eternity that had just passed.

Within a week of returning home from Ireland, I was let go from my job without any warning, after 13 years. My first thought was, I am sober.

I must have sent out 100 resumes to every client I knew and any email connection I found, daily. I didn't get even a phone call for four months. I just kept going to more meetings, staying sober and helping other alcoholics, sometimes just by listening.

I also took any odd job that was offered me. I became an expert at painting, and at installing laminate floors and baseboards. No job was beneath me, and I found physical labor fun after sitting behind a desk for 20 years.

After four months of not getting any bites for employment in my chosen profession, I surrendered to the idea that I might be a general laborer forever. Then a friend said her company was looking for radio testers. She asked if I'd be interested.

I am in my seventh month as a contract engineer. My contract ends in December, but I am staying where my feet are.

All my preconceived notions of what should be shut out the possibility of a Higher Power's intervention. For me, these 24 hours are beyond my wildest dreams. I plan for tomorrow, but not at the expense of wasting today. I am a satisfied customer of AA.

LAURA W.
Fort Lauderdale, Florida

CHAPTER 7

SOBER, GRATEFUL, BROKE

The big and small coincidences (or maybe miracles) that carry recovering alcoholics through tough economic times

"All of us in recovery experience fear of economic insecurity. It's a part of the devastation of the past," writes the author of one of these stories about financial hardship. He took eight years to make a $90,000 financial amends to the government, and as he is congratulated on his last payment, he feels the Promises coming true in his life. Others write of big and small coincidences, or maybe miracles, that have carried them through rough economic times. One member writes about how he used to put big bills in the Seventh Tradition basket when he had a good job. No more; he's now unemployed and there's little to spare. "I recently visited a food bank for the first time in my life," he writes. "But I remain sober and grateful."

Tax Man DECEMBER 2009

She walked into my office, badge in hand. "I'm from the Internal Revenue Service and I need to speak with the doctor," she said. I was summoned from a treatment room and we shook hands as we walked back to my desk.

She wore a business suit and was clearly a no-nonsense person. Glasses perched halfway down her nose, she gazed over them into my eyes. She pulled out an official-looking document and handed it to me.

"Doctor," she said, "I am here to inform you of your unpaid tax liabilities and penalties of $110,000. Because of this amount I have come here to padlock your office as we initiate proceedings against you."

I felt my knees buckle and a deep nausea. Fear gripped me but I reacted calmly ... at least externally. Softly, I said, "If you close my doors, patients will go wanting for treatment and I will have no way at all to repay my tax debt. But if you let me stay open, I promise I'll pay back every cent I owe."

I had been lost in my disease to a point where I was on the verge of losing my family, my home and my practice. I'd found less responsible things to do with my dwindling money supply than pay taxes or bills, saving most of my cash for my bar tab. Our state medical board had done an intervention and had sent me to a five-month treatment facility in Georgia.

I'd sold my house to pay for treatment and lived in a small apartment as I struggled to put my life in some reasonable order. In the six months since I'd been back from Georgia I had incurred other financial obligations. Bill collectors circled like vultures. I had conveniently "forgotten" to pay them, too—and now this.

The agent must have seen the sincerity in my eyes. "I'm not closing you down right now," she said. "I'm going to schedule you to meet with our regional agent in charge of delinquent taxes." She returned the document to her briefcase, nodded solemnly and left.

Within a week I received a letter from the regional agent, setting up an appointment. Boy, did I go to a lot of AA meetings! I hadn't been in recovery long enough to experience the Promises, so I was terrified.

On the scheduled day, I sat across the table from the agent, a sandy-haired man in his late 30s. Although he smiled easily, I knew in a moment he meant business.

"Tell me why you haven't paid your taxes for the last four years," he opened. No small talk here.

With as much clarity as my nervousness could muster, I explained my rapid descent. At first, I had turned to alcohol—and other substances—to quell deep emotional pain and insecurity. Later, I drank to escape any feelings whatsoever. I could see in his eyes that he had never talked to an alcoholic or addict willing to share honestly about the experience.

"You're aware that you owe the government $110,000 in back taxes and penalties, aren't you? You told our field agent you are willing to pay back every cent? How do you plan to do this?"

I responded, "I have no idea. I haven't a penny to my name."

He tapped the table with his pencil, concentrating. "Jeff, I want you to write down the experience you've just related to me. And I want you to inventory every possession you have and your monthly living expenses."

I did what I was told. I scoured the little apartment, inventorying all my earthly goods. I wrote out my history of alcoholism; it felt like a Fourth Step. And I listed my expenses. Then we met. Slowly he read my story and he reviewed my assets and expenses.

"Jeff, I feel that your alcoholism can be viewed by the IRS as an illness. Because of this, I'm removing $20,000 in penalties from what you owe." I swallowed hard as I took this in. "Here's how we'll deal with the remaining $90,000 of your tax debt. We will allow

$10 a day for food (this was 25 years ago) and a total of $600 a month for rent and all your other expenses. You will write us a check for the balance of your net income each month until your debt is paid."

I could continue to practice! I had a chance to make it financially. I knew with the help of my recovery program and support of my staff and friends I could do this; I could work through my obligations.

Because of my limited funds, I began riding an old bicycle for exercise. Soon, I rode everywhere. The days when I knew I didn't have hospital rounds or house calls, I rode to work. My cycling helped me through those lean years. This cheap transportation not only got me where I wanted to go, but also helped my body heal physically, emotionally and spiritually. I could go to meetings anywhere without worrying about car expenses unbalancing my meager budget.

Each month I dutifully calculated my net income, paid myself my $600 salary, and wrote the IRS a check for the balance. Each month I went through feelings of anger and resentment at the government, the medical board, my disease and, finally, myself.

Day after day I attended meetings, soaking up lessons of acceptance and honesty. I listened to stories of people in much worse shape than me finding hope to make it through one more day. Eventually a glimmer of gratitude started to glow and I accepted responsibility for my financial position.

Over the years, my anger and resentments faded. My tax obligation was still in the thousands, but a weight was being lifted. I started to know I was going to be okay. Fear of financial insecurity was leaving. Time takes time; this particular time took eight years. I worked and went to hundreds of meetings.

One day the sandy-haired agent appeared in my office and pulled out an envelope. "This is yours," he said. "You might like to frame it." I teased it open. A light-green government check for $1,000 beamed up at me.

"You overshot your last payment to us. You've done it. You've paid off your entire obligation of $90,000. Congratulations!"

My eyes teared up. He shook my hand and, before he could step back, found himself in a bear hug. Over the years, we had become friends.

In those eight years other financial challenges had also been met. My practice stabilized. My staff, who had hung with me and had accepted meager salaries those long years, all received raises. I put myself on a salary and budget. And I made sure my number one financial priority was to meet all tax obligations—on time!

All of us in recovery experience fear of economic insecurity. It's a part of the devastation of the past. But, truly, the Promises do come true.

JEFF W.
Milwaukie, Oregon

New Boots MARCH 2010

At six months of sobriety, I began to feel as though my life wasn't progressing forward fast enough. I began to lose my willingness to accept life on life's terms. I was working as a pizza delivery person and I was the proud owner of a pair of boots that had seen better days.

I was at work one evening and, while work was slow, I tried to repair my boots by gluing strips of leather between the sole and the separated toe. It held briefly, then soon fell apart. I started to realize that I had to accept that these boots were a lost cause.

Not only were they my only pair of boots, they were my only pair of shoes.

I sat in my car, opened up my Big Book to "Acceptance Was the Answer," and read the entire story. As I finished, I was told that I had a delivery. I got the pies and headed out.

I ended up behind a transit bus that was moving at about 20 mph. I started pounding on my dashboard and tailgated the bus. Then I remembered what I had just read a few minutes earlier, and backed off. I took several deep breaths and told myself I had no control over that bus driver.

The bus passed a bus stop. Since I'd backed off, I got a good view of the bus stop. It was empty except for a pair of boots just sitting there. I stopped and picked up the boots; they were brand new. I stood there for a moment, and then I shouted, "Do these boots belong to anyone?"

There was no one around, so I put them in my front seat and continued on with my delivery. I made the delivery and returned to my car. That's when I noticed that the boots were my exact size. I took the insoles of my old boots out and placed them inside the new pair, then slipped my feet inside. I thought, My God, I have new boots!

I called and told my sponsor what had happened. I asked if it was right for me to keep them. He said, "It sounds as though God left you a pair of new boots."

BRENT A.
Atlanta, Georgia

No Spares OCTOBER 2010

(From Dear Grapevine)

In response to "Basket Case" (July 2010), I applaud the largesse of those who are able and willing to place large contributions in the basket. When I first attended AA many years ago, I aped the others there, most of whom placed change in the "hat" (and it often was an actual hat). Years later, when I had secured a good job, I occasionally gave a fiver out of gratitude. Today, I am among the ranks of the many unemployed, and often simply do not have a buck or two to spare. I recently visited a food bank for the first time in my life. But I remain sober and grateful.

COREY B.
Long Beach, California

Gimme Shelter MARCH 2010

After living rurally for six years with my two daughters, it became necessary for me to move back to Christchurch, New Zealand. I had eight weeks to prepare for moving and I looked at many homes. They far exceeded what I could afford. My past behavior, when looking for property, was to rent what I wanted and get the nicest home, despite the burden it would cause the family financially. This time my thoughts had changed. I could not afford to rent anything that I had viewed so far. Doing so would take the food from our bellies, clothing from our backs and heat from our bodies during the bitter winter months: my thoughtless actions would cripple the family.

I put the problem in my Higher Power's hands and I put my name down on a government listing for a home. My need wasn't considered urgent and I could be waiting at least a year before a place became available. "Keep us informed," said the housing officer, "of any changes to your circumstances." I kept up my search for a property.

Several incidents occurred. My estranged husband, actively alcoholic and suicidal, went missing; my car's gearbox failed; and my oldest daughter was in a car accident. She had missed payments on her insurance. Also, my elderly mother fell. As I kept notifying the housing officer of the changes in my affairs, I felt his looks of disbelief.

One morning I awoke and crumbled inside. I just couldn't face another day. I called out to God in tears, "I cannot do this anymore. It's too big for me. Please, I give it all to you!" I did my daily readings and my prayer and meditation. I felt a peace and comfort within me that was hard to explain.

I continued doing what was in front of me. The police found my husband safe in his mother's home, after a four-day bender. We rented a car and I sold my car, getting a very good price for it. My daughter's car went in for repair and negotiations began with the insurance company. I still had not found a home, and the day arrived to move. At the last minute, I found affordable accommodations for us: a tent site just around the road from my mother. We were going to stay in my four-person tent and experience a new adventure. The park had all the amenities that we required, plus the bonus of a playground and a swimming pool. Our belongings went into storage. The move into the tent changed our situation on the housing list—we rose into the urgent register because a tent wasn't permanent housing.

We'd been living comfortably in the tent for six days when my mother died. Prior to my recovery from alcoholism, she and I could not be in the same room for more than five minutes without fighting. But with 14 years' sobriety, I could be with her and do for her what I should have done for so many years.

Over the weekend, I did what was needed with my family and returned each night to the tent with my girls. Several people had offered to house us, but I turned them down. The moments since my mother died were the closest I'd had with the girls. I wanted to stay just where we were. We cried, we laughed, and we shared stories about my mother, their grandmother. It was a beautiful time together in the tent.

When I rang the housing officer to tell him that my mother had died, he said he would do all he could for me. Half an hour later, he called: We had a home. It was too small, but I was going to take what was provided. Then he called back: Another home was available, this time with exactly the requirements I had requested from the agency. Without hesitation, I said, "I'll take it."

I know today that because I kept walking the road of recovery with joy and love, accepting and giving thanks, we were provided for.

I am still in this lovely home. I have landscaped the property with a backyard garden and an area of fruit trees and spring bulbs in remembrance of my mother. With this experience, I truly made the decision to turn my will and my life over to the care of God, and then I got out of the way.

JENNIFER P.
Christchurch, New Zealand

The Trap Door AUGUST 1996

It was just before my second anniversary when my husband and I separated. He was getting sober at a sober house, and I was left with the care of our four children. My landlord had lost the house to the bank, which was evicting me. I couldn't afford to rent anyplace else on my welfare grant so I had no choice but to join the ranks of the homeless welfare mothers who put up at a motel in a neighboring town.

Meanwhile, I was suffering with untreated acute depression. I saw little point in living, much less staying sober. I thought that I was a bad mother for what my children and I were about to go through. I thought my children would be better off without me. My sponsor at that time was afraid that I would harm myself and urged me to go to the emergency room. I refused. I felt that if I could just talk about my bad feelings I could make it the two days I had left before my scheduled doctor's appointment. She asked me to call other people.

In my frazzled state of mind, I thought that meant that she didn't want to listen to me anymore. I thought that I was too sick even for AA. I felt so hopeless. For almost two years, people had been telling me, "Keep coming, it gets better," but my life was only getting worse. When my sponsor asked me to call other people, I felt she'd abandoned me at the very time that I needed her most. I was afraid to reach out to anyone else. I tried. I called people and let them know what was going on with me. But I really felt unworthy and alone.

Three days later was moving day. I hadn't slept. I was now being treated for my depression, but I'd only been on the medication for one day. I was an emotional and physical wreck. I had wonderful people from my home group coming to help me move and I couldn't think straight. An Al-Anon friend had generously donated her basement for storage. Another Al-Anon friend came to help me with the move. When I told her that my brain was fried, she took over for me. She told everyone what to do, what to take where, and when to take it. I had such a sense of desolation and loss as I watched all my worldly possessions removed from my home of four years and loaded onto trucks (even though these trucks had bumper stickers telling me "Easy Does It" and "One Day at a Time"). When my Al-Anon friend had to go, she handed over her job as foreman to an AA friend who oversaw the final emptying of my house.

That night, as I tucked my children into bed at the "Hell Motel," I thanked God for another day of sobriety. I thanked God for both programs, AA and Al-Anon, and the friends who'd so generously donated their time, trucks, muscle, and space. It wasn't too hard to stay sober that day because I'd been surrounded by members of my home group. It was the next few days that were rough.

I was the only one at the motel who was sober. There was a drug dealer across the hall and a few active crack users. Those who weren't using drugs were drinking. I couldn't blame them. If I wasn't sober already, I would have been just as loaded as they were. It was very tempting to take a drink. I had the perfect excuse for a relapse. Poor me! No one would blame me. I couldn't call my sponsor and I was afraid to ask anyone else to sponsor me. I had no one to turn to. Sure, I called people, but I held back because I didn't want to overwhelm anyone by describing to them what I was going through. I felt like the condemned prisoner on the hangman's scaffold with the noose around my neck. But when the trap door below my feet opened up, a miracle happened. Instead of drinking and dying, I was caught in the loving and capable hands of my Higher Power.

It was during this time when I really learned that my Higher

Power loved me. I certainly didn't keep myself sober. Instead, I was granted a daily reprieve. I asked for help in the morning, even though some days I really didn't want to stay sober. I went to meetings and used the meetings as my sponsor. I voiced my gratitude every night for another day of sobriety. Gradually, I began to look around me at all of the sick and suffering people at the motel. I saw the effects of their active disease on their children. I became truly grateful for this unmerited gift of sobriety. One of the women whom I used to watch drink was watching me too. We began to talk about drinking. I shared my story with her. I invited her to meetings and she came! We drank coffee together and talked throughout the day. She couldn't get more than three or four days together at a time, but I stayed sober. I don't know where she is today, but I will never forget her. God put us together to keep me sober. I hope she is sober today; I know I'm delighted and amazed that I am. Sobriety is a precious gift from God. Who am I to turn down a gift from God?

SUSIE K.
Yarmouthport, Massachusetts

The Woman in the Mirror JUNE 1998
(From Dear Grapevine)

My first glimpse of AA started at age twenty-one when the drinking buddy I'd so naively married ended up in treatment. We both attended a meeting that combined AA and Al-Anon. I couldn't admit I was alcoholic but an alcoholic woman at this meeting left a big impression on me. She had such confidence and beamed and smiled at everyone. My soul ached for what she had, but I couldn't admit our common problem: alcohol.

At age twenty-two I stumbled into an AA clubhouse after a nine-day binge. This period of sobriety didn't last long because I also discovered, after being transported to the state hospital, that I was manic-depressive, and being alcoholic and having this mental illness was too much to digest. So I gave up AA. After my final drunk, which had failed to produce a happy evening because I couldn't get enough alcohol, I once again entertained the idea of AA.

Pregnant with my daughter and raising a one-year-old son, I knew I had to do something, so I decided to go to AA for Lent. I continued going even though I saw my marriage self-destruct, as my husband became ever more abusive. The longer I was sober the more my husband drank. I think he would have rather seen me dead than sober.

Even though I was very afraid, I left the marriage for a welfare check at a year of sobriety. It was a step up in the world because we had started to starve. I didn't quit the meetings after this even though money was tight and sitters were expensive. My sobriety was worth every penny.

Thank God the AA program requires progress, not perfection, or I would have given up. I used the Big Book as my guide because I knew my way had gotten me in the mess I was trying to get out of. The more faith I acquired the more I turned things over to the God of my understanding. I sometimes wondered if all the hell I had gone through trying to stay sober had only given me something to keep coming back to complain about!

All of a sudden the day came when the members of AA started giving me compliments on how I was doing, and the smiles I returned were genuine because I knew I was doing better. I could finally face the woman in the mirror and smile and be absolutely overwhelmed by gratitude toward God and the members of AA. I've discovered from spending lots of time with myself that God has blessed me with many talents. At times I wonder if I resemble that confident, serene woman I looked up to at my first meeting a long time ago. I certainly feel like her, and that counts for everything.

MICHELLE V.
Mandan, North Dakota

PART FOUR
SPIRITUAL ADVERSITY

CHAPTER 8
THE END OF THE JOURNEY

Realizing that their days are soon drawing to a close, these AAs reaffirm their desire to stay sober

When these AAs get the devastating news that their illness may be fatal, they call on their Higher Power, gather the Fellowship around them for support, and keep on taking it one day at a time. One member, dealt an inoperable cancer, knows that it is as important for him to die sober as it is to live sober. "The Twelve Steps ... are called 'a design for living.' Can the Steps also be called 'a design for dying?' I do believe so." Many of us, as we get older in the program, could face this ourselves—these stories are examples of AAs who have found acceptance. "I have a list on my computer of the AA members I've known who have gone on to that big meeting in the sky," writes a member who's had heart bypass surgery, cancer, an aneurysm, cataract surgery and chronic obstructive pulmonary disease yet still attends his home group every Monday night. "I'll see you at the meeting."

Just an Attitude APRIL 2002

After a recent visit to the hospital, I was told that I not only had colon cancer, but that it had spread to three places on my liver. The news was pretty devastating. The hospital is one of the leading medical institutions in the country, so the word from its staff that this was practically not treatable was not very comforting. Thank God for AA. Ten-and-a-half years ago, I would not be handling this nearly as well as I think I am. If I had made it this far, I most certainly would be too drunk to feel anything. Today, I have the wonderful opportunity to demonstrate that I practice what I have preached. I go to as many meetings as I can. I have absolutely no desire for alcohol. I pray that the God of my understanding will use me even more in the months that remain and that I will be able to apply the St. Francis Prayer found in the Eleventh Step.

A fact that leaps out at me is that it is not one day at a time—it is now moment by moment. I certainly do not wish to mess up today by worrying about what will happen tomorrow, or live in that abyss of despair over the past. That would really be stupid in my book. Having had this revelation, I intensely want to share it with those out there who are teetering on the brink of sobriety. What you are throwing away is the "now." Living a sober life is not easy, but it is simple. We do it together in AA.

One thing that I say repeatedly in meetings is that in every black cloud there is a silver lining. Ever since learning of my situation, I have been on a quest for silver linings.

When I first received the news, my wife was there in the room with me. The pain that registered on my wife's face was unmistakable. I wish that I could have taken that pain from her, but it was clearly the result of her love for me. My daughter was also with us, and I saw much the same reaction from her. The love that shone through the pain was definitely a silver lining. I was not a very lovable drunk. I did not deserve any of this! I had a nine-day stay in the hospital resulting from an operation to by-pass the tumor. I had a steady stream of visitors. I really did not know that so many people loved and cared for me. God blessed me tenfold—another silver lining! The other day after a meeting, a friend said to me, "I just hope that I can mean as much to someone else in their life as you have meant in mine." Now my ego could run wild with that one. But AA has drilled into me that this is only my God working through me.

Another one of those moments of clarity hit me when I realized that with the clock ticking like it is I do not have time for anger, resentment, or self-pity. Time is far too precious. My desire to share has greatly intensified. With gifts like these, I have begun to wonder if my situation is not an opportunity rather than a problem.

I believe that a problem is not a problem, it's an attitude. Without that, it's just a situation, and the solution is always adjusting that attitude. That is the first line of defense. The AA way of life applies in all our affairs as we trudge the road to happy destiny.

JULIAN O.
Durham, North Carolina

Living Sober, Dying Sober

SEPTEMBER 2004

(Excerpt)

After years of practicing the Twelve Steps, learning prayer and meditation, and helping others, my life was going rather smoothly. I was living sober.

Then recently, I was hit with a double, or you might even say triple, whammy—prostate and bladder cancer, kidney problems, and a heart attack.

Consultation with professionals led to the conclusion that surgery and other heroic measures would not be used. I am now at the point of dying sober. This is as important to me as living sober. So, what do I do? The Twelve Steps of Alcoholics Anonymous, of course. They are called "a design for living." Can the Steps also be called "a design for dying?" I do believe so.

I started with Step One, and the admission and acceptance of my powerlessness. Then Step Two and surrender to the powers of nature, which are far greater than my powers. Then the Third Step Prayer, in my own words: "God, I really do turn my will and my life over to your care." After saying this prayer with my spiritual confidant, I continued with an inventory of myself, as I am at this point in time.

Then, I admitted to God, to another person, and to myself, the exact nature of my wrongs so I could identify what needed to be changed in my attitude and behavior from now on. Time is growing short, so I went on to Step Six, where I got ready for God to remove the bothersome stuff. Then came the Seventh Step Prayer, that my shortcomings would be removed.

Of course, when God removes my shortcomings, this leaves me with a big void unless I have something to put in their place. Here is where I turn to what I call "Step Seven-and-a-half" for relief. To substitute good for bad, I go to the Prayer of St. Francis in *Twelve Steps and Twelve Traditions* for corrective measures.

The Tenth and Eleventh Steps I call "maintenance Steps." I now practice these through daily prayer and meditation as recommended by Anne S. (Dr. Bob's wife) and the early AAs.

All of the above has led me to a spiritual awakening. I have had a complete change of attitude and behavior sufficient to carry me on to the final trudge along the Road of Happy Destiny. I am daily sharing experience, strength, and hope with others as we follow Dr. Bob's suggestion to clean house, trust God, and help others.

How to do this is explained to me in the final pages of the story

"AA Taught Him to Handle Sobriety" in the Third Edition of the Big Book. Among other things, we are told that in AA "we reject fantasizing and ... embrace reality with open arms." This leads me to where I want to be at the end of my journey along the broad highway, walking hand in hand with God, and being at peace with myself and with others.

I am convinced that death is a part of life, just as birth is. I truly feel that everything in my life—people, places, things—have been "on loan" to me. I came into life with only love, and I am going out with only love. I am really looking forward to the experience of passing out of this world with gratitude for having the AA program and Fellowship freely given to me by those who have passed this way before. How grateful I am that the founders of AA followed the advice they gave everyone else to "pass it on."

Fear of death has been relieved by faith and courage. There's a lot of stuff written about how to live sober, and my advice to you is to read and contemplate what is there, get a sponsor, go to meetings, help the newcomer, and pray. And one day, maybe you'll be as lucky as I am. Maybe someday, by applying our Twelve Steps, you will reach the point at which you are at peace with yourself, with others, and with God. You'll have the privilege of dying sober.

BILL M.
Midland, Michigan

Serenity Garden SEPTEMBER 2010

Today, I am acutely aware of the miracles that I have experienced in my life and have witnessed in the lives of others since I came through the doors of Alcoholics Anonymous. There is no question that God, as I understand God, is the source of these miracles. I am also aware of the beauty and magic that surrounds me and this awareness, I believe, has been a gift from the young people who have touched my life. It is as if God and those young people are threads woven together making a beautiful design for my life's tapestry.

As I reflect on the miracles of my 24 years of sobriety, I also consider another deadly disease that I have survived. In April 2007, I was diagnosed with pancreatic cancer. Because of the size of the inoperable tumor the prognosis looked as if I would live for only a few months.

When the news reached two young people whom I sponsor, they sprang into action. Ron L. and Anne P. called to say they would be picking me up for a trip to Bernheim Forest, about two hours from my home in Frankfort, Ky. They selected a picnic table surrounded by beautiful blooming dogwood trees. They covered the table with a fine linen tablecloth and set it with china, silver and crystal. The gourmet meal was delicious. The day was magical.

The following week, Ron traveled to the mountains of Brazil to visit a great healer who lived there. He presented my case along with my picture, and visited the healer's compound for 11 days of prayer and meditation for me. He returned with herbs and a hope that I would live.

A third biopsy showed that I have a rare cancer that is slow-growing. So after 30 radiation treatments I decided to keep a commitment to teach for a year at a university in North Carolina. As I taught those classes and interacted with the students, my energy began to return.

A group of the students asked if they could meet at my house one evening a week to discuss various topics about life in general. It's difficult to explain the special connection I have with my students. It was as if God were giving me the opportunity to make a living amends to students in my past who were enrolled in my classes when I had been drinking before I entered the room to lecture.

After returning home to Kentucky, I have continued to keep in touch with many of the North Carolina students, as well as those I met in AA there. I continue to attend at least three meetings a week here in my home group, work individually with the people I sponsor, and meet with them as a group twice a month.

I am writing this article as I sit in what I call my "Serenity Garden." AA has taught me that I have only this day, this moment. When I focus on the beautiful gifts in my garden—the flowers and trees are my gifts from God; the statues and angels are my gifts from the young people in AA—I realize how very blessed I am. I am so grateful for the miracles I have received from God and for the magic from my young friends.

KIZZIE P.
Frankfort, Kentucky

Grace and Dignity SEPTEMBER 2004
(From Dear Grapevine)

Bill M.'s "Living Sober, Dying Sober" in the September 2004 issue was inspiring and thought-provoking, especially in light of where I'm at in this journey of life. Soon I'll be 81. I was 47 when the plug went in the jug. Bill M. described medical problems as being hit with "whammies." I can really relate. During the past twelve years I've had some major stuff—heart bypass surgery, cancer, an aneurysm, cataract surgery and chronic obstructive pulmonary disease which requires oxygen therapy. In spite of all the "whammies," I still attend my home group meeting every Monday night. I play golf if the weather isn't too hot or humid, and I walk the aisles of the local "super center" on a regular basis. Of course, I'm not planning on dying anytime soon—only the good Lord knows the ending. But, as you may have guessed, I don't buy green bananas anymore, either!

I share this with the readers because at meetings I've often heard the myth that maybe 50 percent of us die drunk. Don't you believe it! We all have the privilege of dying sober, as Bill M. did. It's really a simple process—to practice the principles on a daily basis in all my affairs. I have a list on my computer of the AA members I've known who have gone on to that big meeting in the sky. The total from that list today is seventy-two and the great news is that all but just six died sober. "Dying Sober" will happen if I work at it. I plan to! I'll see you at the meeting.

DON A.
Lakeview, Arkansas

No Excuse to Drink AUGUST 1996

One frightful summer day at the beginning of June 1995 I was diagnosed with breast cancer. I equated cancer with death and felt that at thirty-seven years of age, I was too young to die. Fearful thoughts raced through my head. The committee was in full force and it wouldn't give me any peace. My body felt as tight as a rubber band stretched to the breaking point.

The doctor said I'd need a mastectomy and probably chemotherapy afterward. I listened to him relate my prognosis to my family and all at once I decided I couldn't cope with this news. I needed a drink and some Valium fast (even though I've never had any Valium in my life). These circumstances justified chemical relief and I said as much to my mother. I decided that dealing with cancer was a big deal and that my sobriety was going to have to take a back seat for a while. I also said I was going to let go of all the women I was sponsoring, so I could concentrate on me. I still can't believe how quickly my thinking became stinking, even with seven years of sobriety.

A Higher Power must have been looking out for me, realizing that this was too big for me to deal with alone. My sponsor called me. It seems my mother had been concerned and called her. We talked and cried for a long time. She suggested I call her sponsor who, as it turns out, had had the same surgery and chemotherapy about eleven years before. She had six years of sobriety at the time and told me how she had coped. She suggested that I stay close to meetings, share about what was going on, and not let go of any sponsees because they would turn out to be a blessing. She told me that as long as I stayed closed to God, the Fellowship, and the Twelve Steps, I'd be just fine. She gave me hope, the same kind of hope AA members gave me when I first tried to stop drinking. All of a sudden, I knew in my heart I didn't have to do this alone and that there were others ahead of me to light the way, just like with my sobriety.

It's now been eight months since my mastectomy. I was out of work for seven months while having four surgeries and five months of chemotherapy. The Fellowship, God, and the Steps did truly carry me. People brought meetings to my house or drove me to them when I was unable to drive so I was usually able to make a minimum of three meetings a week, no matter how sick I was. Fellow members loved me even when all my hair fell out and I lost fifteen pounds. Sponsees brought me groceries, made my bed, and held my hand. I've never felt so loved in all my life.

The God that I came to believe in while reading the Big Book was there during the darkest hours to give me courage and strength when no human power could. I was even asked to lead a Step series of meetings to share my experience, strength, and hope on the Steps. This helped greatly in keeping me focused on the solution and out of myself. Instead of letting go of my sponsees, I actually started sponsoring two more women. It gave me tremendous joy to know I could help and inspire others even during my own trying times.

I'm happy to report my sobriety date remains the same. I found that even dealing with "the big C" was no excuse to drink. I now know what they mean when they say, "There are no big deals."

DEBBIE B.
Hollywood, Florida

Another Chance JUNE 2003

(From Dear Grapevine)

Back in June 2001, the Grapevine published my article "Bart's Last Chance," and I was very proud that it had been selected. I've been asked questions about it on quite a few occasions. Not "Aren't you too old to ride a motorcycle?" or "Weren't you in a slippery place in the nude bar?" but "How did you react when the doctors told you that you had two kinds of cancer?" and the one in every Grade-B movie, "How long do I got, Doc?"

There is no doubt that cancer comes down like a tornado. I went through the entire gamut of emotions: denial, anger, bargaining, depression, and, finally, acceptance, where all those meetings, readings, sponsoring, and Twelfth-Step work kicked in and recovery began.

After two bone marrow biopsies, my doctor called my wife and me into his office. "Are you religious people?" he asked. My mind jumped into fast-forward. The next few sentences were blurs. Then I shifted into anger and denial: "I gave up booze seventeen years ago! I gave up cigarettes twelve years ago! Why me?" The doctor said, "You ought to be grateful for stopping the abuse to your body. Had you not given up those drugs, we could not give you chemotherapy to stop this cancerous aggression." The thought struck me dumb. Yes, I am grateful that I stopped using those poisons, stopped living so close to the edge, stopped drunken driving, and started a better way of living.

When I first was diagnosed with cancer, I did ask, "How long do I got, Doc?" His reply was, "Six months without treatment or a year with." That was May 5, 1998. This May 5, 2003, I'll have enjoyed five years of special time with my family and friends, and for this, I am eternally grateful.

BART G.
Montello, Wisconsin

Living Sober APRIL 2001

(From Dear Grapevine)

I was twelve years sober in June 1999, when I received a disturbing diagnosis from my doctor: it was cancer. I was in shock. With my best alcoholic thinking, I thought I would die in a couple of weeks. I was wrong. The doctor told me I might live a year or longer, but I was already planning the funeral. It was going to be a big AA memorial service with all my friends and family there; I would see to that!

I fell into a depression and told my husband that I would have to leave him behind soon. I also started giving away clothes and stuff from my apartment. Why leave it all until the end?

Then I went to my home group and shared the news with them. I was most grateful for the response. People sent cards, offered sympathy, and when we moved to another apartment to save money, AA members helped.

Sobriety and AA have helped me through this trying year. I discovered that you can live with cancer. I did not know that. I had thought that once you had a diagnosis it was immediate death. Thank God, I am still sober. I do my Third Step Prayer every day and I aim to do God's will for as long as I have on Earth.

LAURA W.
San Diego, California

CHAPTER 9

THROUGH MANY DARK VALLEYS

Money problems, health problems, relationship problems—
AAs have the tools to face any adversity life hands them

We can't control the cards life deals us. But we can control how we respond to them. As the stories in this book show, AA members have the power to make it through any tough time, any problem, sober. And some, as shown in this chapter, claim they no longer have problems. "I had so many problems for such a long time," the author of the appropriately named "A Life Without Problems" writes. "Where did they go? The short (but somewhat mysterious) answer is: the Third Step swept them away. I turned my will and my life over to the care of God, as I understand him." It's through the Third Step ... meetings ... prayer and meditation ... and working with others ... that AAs reach a solution. "Between God and AA, I can get through any situation as long as I don't pick up that first drink," says the author of "How the Universe Works." These stories show how AAs have come to accept hard times by using the tools of the program.

Size 8, Extra Wide JANUARY 2001

At first glance, the shoe did not appear to be any kind of a solution. It was dirty, worn out, beat up, and hopelessly flawed. Initially, it didn't do anything to lessen my misery. I put my face back in my hands and continued to cry.

I should have been the happiest man alive. I was surrounded by pristine wilderness in a remote area of Yellowstone National Park. I was employed as a chemical dependency counselor for a Montana treatment center specializing in treating young men between the ages of fifteen and twenty-one. Most of the youth I worked with had long histories of alcohol and drug abuse and trouble with the law. Many had been physically and/or sexually abused. It was hard, draining work, but I loved it. I was working with younger versions of myself.

After several years in a brutal reform school, I had emerged an angry, bitter young man. Then chronic alcoholism took its toll, and I spent the next few years in and out of jails and institutions. I almost killed my daughter in a car accident while I was drunk and, consequently, lost custody of her. My self-loathing was outdone only by my self-pity. By the age of twenty-five, I was just another skid row derelict with no front teeth. I wanted nothing to do with God. I always felt dirty, and if I didn't have a current excuse, I could always recall what had happened in reform school or what I had done to my daughter, Sheri, to justify how I felt about myself.

Alcoholics Anonymous rescued me at the age of twenty-eight. I was welcomed into a loving home group, and with the help of a tough sponsor, I began to work the Steps and develop a spiritual life. I made slow progress. Although almost immediately my life began to improve, it took me years to get off the streets permanently. I married and moved to Montana, where I went to work for a treatment center. I was the happiest that I had ever been, but I still carried a lot of baggage. I had deep depressions, which came on with no warning and lasted for weeks. I still was filled with tremendous remorse from my past. I had horrible nightmares and sometimes would wake up in the night screaming and covered with cold sweat. A physiologist said I suffered from post-traumatic stress syndrome from all the violence I had experienced in reform school and on the street. I had enormous financial wreckage that weighed on me constantly. And although I desperately wanted to establish a relationship with my daughter, she wanted nothing to do with me. I didn't blame her, but it still hurt.

All too often, I felt as though my job and my new life in Montana were just flukes or a cosmic joke. Sooner or later, it would all come crashing down and I would return to skid row where I belonged.

It was in that frame of mind that I prepared for an upcoming wilderness survival trip with my young clients. On impulse, I attempted to lift my spirits by purchasing a new pair of hiking shoes. At least my feet would feel good.

The wilderness trip went badly from the beginning. From our drop-off point, we went almost straight up over a mountain range, so we were all stiff and sore after a couple of days. My group was a difficult one. It was hard enough to keep them from beating up one another, much less participate in the therapy. I wasn't making much headway with them, and the farther up into the mountains we got, the lower my spirits sank.

To make matters worse, my new shoes were giving me blisters. On day four, a manufacturing defect in one of the shoes became apparent and it began to self-destruct. It became increasingly painful to walk in, and by the time we set up camp that evening, I was in agony.

That night in my tent, I took stock of my situation. The shoe was not repairable; I had no way to call out for help and no one in my group had brought along extra footwear of any kind. I considered finishing the trip barefoot, but in the rugged terrain, with a sixty-plus-pound pack on my back, I knew my feet would be in shreds in no time. I would just have to endure the pain of wearing the shoe and pray it would hold together six more days.

The following morning, we geared up and hit the trail. Within a few minutes, my foot was killing me. Consumed with self-pity, I began to think not only about the shoe problem, but also about all my other problems. My mood got darker. The shoe got worse. Every step was excruciating. I began to get angry. The shoe disintegrated. I exploded. Screaming profanities, I threw my pack on the ground. I became overwhelmed with feelings of hopelessness. That shoe seemed to represent my entire life—self-destructive and irreparable. I sat down on the trail, put my face in my hands, and began to cry.

Slowly I became aware of some commotion. Then one of the boys began shaking my shoulder.

"Kevin, look. Look what I found. It was lying over in the bushes," he said.

I glanced up and saw he had a shoe in his hands. I went back to my crying. He was persistent and shook me again.

"Take a look at it. Check it out."

Drying my eyes, I looked at the shoe. The first thing I noticed was that it was in bad shape. The eyelets were rusted, and the tongue was frayed. There was a big hole in the toe, and when I turned it over I saw that the tread was worn almost flat. It felt stiff, the way leather gets when weathered without protection. It looked as if it had lain there for a long time. The second thing I noticed was that it was for a left foot, the same as my problem shoe. I looked closer. I have short, wide feet—size 8, triple E. I have trouble finding my size in shoe stores. This shoe was short and wide. I slipped it on. It not only fit, it felt comfortable. I could feel grooves in the sole that someone's toes had worn in over time. They fit my toes perfectly.

We all stared at one another for a time, speechless; then hoisting our packs we continued down the trail. I stared at the shoe as I hiked. Where did it come from? It had obviously been there a long time. There was only one shoe; we had looked for its mate and hadn't found it. Left foot. My size. If my shoe had come apart ten yards sooner or ten yards later, we would have missed it.

I realized that my Higher Power was telling me he loved me and would take care of me. I was overwhelmed with gratitude. The rest of the trip went without a hitch. By the end, all the blisters on my left foot had healed, while my right foot continued to blister.

It has been twelve years since that trip, yet the shoe continues to have an impact on my life and the lives of others. Sometimes when working with a new man who is overwhelmed with the wreckage of his past, I pull the shoe off my bookshelf and share my small miracle. It always has an uplifting effect.

AA has worked miracles in my life. I have been reunited with my daughter, and we are the best of friends. I was with her at the birth of our grandson, Timmy, and with her when she had emergency surgery at the University of Washington to remove a life-threatening tumor. After several years, I was able to earn enough money to pay all my bad debts. God delivered me from my nightmares and cold sweats. My depressions have changed from dark abysses to passing shadows.

Over the years, I've sometimes wondered why God used a beat-up shoe to get my attention. The answer is obvious, but it had evaded me for all these years.

I was asked to speak a few weeks ago. I am used to speaking, but as the day approached I became nervous and apprehensive. I had a new set of difficulties in my life. Our son had been diagnosed with a rare terminal illness. For the first time in many years, I was unemployed and our finances were strained. Some of my old feelings of self-pity and bitterness began to resurface. I could hear the thundering hooves of the four horsemen in the distance. How could I carry the message to others when my own life seemed to be careening out of control again?

As my wife, Helene, and I got ready to leave the house that evening, I noticed the shoe on the bookshelf. I put it in a bag and brought it along.

We stopped at a diner to grab a burger on the way. As we sat waiting for our meal, I put the shoe on the table between us and began to share how inadequate I felt and why. When I finished, we both stared at the shoe. Our waitress brought us our food, but we continued to stare. Then we both started to cry. Our waitress ran over and asked if our food was okay. We laughed and assured her it was. We finished our meal and headed to the meeting, so I could tell them how God had taken a beat-up and extremely flawed shoe and made it useful to carry his message of hope.

KEVIN G.
Juneau, Alaska

A Life Without Problems MAY 2007

(Excerpt)

It's now been over twenty-three years since I joined AA and stopped drinking. Twenty-three years, four marriages, three divorces, nine jobs, fourteen addresses (across four different states), dozens of home groups, and a countless number of meetings. I only offer this list for perspective: The list makes it obvious that I haven't always seen myself as a guy with no problems.

This week I was asked to give a short share at a Solutions meeting. I intended to talk mainly about how much sense Bill W.'s writings on the Third Step made to me these days, especially those contained in Chapter Five of the Big Book. Somewhere along the line, though, I noted that I didn't have any problems at all today.

I wasn't trying to brag or impress anyone. My AA talks are always spontaneous or at least extemporaneous. Before I begin, I ask God to direct my speech. Then I trust that He, She, It, or They will do just that, and I let fly.

Anyway, this particular morning, God (through me) was speaking well. Laughs abounded, heads nodded, side conversations didn't exist. I shared how, having turned my will and my life over to the care of God, I had no problems left. I talked about how, even into my double-digit years of sobriety, I would cling to my problems, make them my identity, attack anyone who might offer to solve them and, in general, fight to stay in my comfortable zone of unhappy competence that I had established with my problems.

After the meeting, a long-time friend of mine asked me earnestly, "How did you do it?" It was a question that I wasn't quite prepared for, and I'm sure my answer to her wasn't very helpful. But her question to me certainly has been.

How did I eliminate my problems? I mean, I had so many problems for such a long time. Where did they go? The short (but somewhat mysterious) answer is: the Third Step swept them away. I turned my will and my life over to the care of God, as I understand him (or don't understand him, her, it or them). Now I have only one task, laid out in AA's Eleventh Step: "praying only for knowledge of His will for us and the power to carry that out."

The rest is no longer any of my business.

Assuming I am willing, exactly how do I turn my will and my life over to the care of God? This question is answered directly in *Twelve Steps and Twelve Traditions*: "We can pause, ask for quiet, and in the stillness simply say, 'God grant me the serenity to accept the things I cannot change, courage to change the things I can, and wisdom to know the difference.'"

I can state it even more bluntly: In this moment, regardless of what happened before or what may happen tomorrow, what is the very best thing I can possibly do, right now?

JIM P.
Santa Monica, California

A Great Loss Made Him Even More Grateful for AA FEBRUARY 1980

(Excerpt)

I got a semi-hysterical phone call from my twenty-two-year-old daughter, my youngest and closest child. She was 1,500 miles away in New Jersey, where she was in college and where I had previously lived and gotten sober. She said that her gynecologist had told her she probably had cancer, that he had scheduled a biopsy. I assured her that I would be there in time to share the news of the test, whether good or bad.

In a state of shock, I headed for the closest AA meeting I could find, accompanied by a trusted AA friend. I was relieved to discover that a severe blow, such as I had just received, gave me an insatiable craving for a meeting rather than for a drink; but I was too numb to fully appreciate my reactions and to thank God that AA was there to turn to, rather than the bottle.

Pulling myself together, I packed my clothes, said goodbye to my wife, and flew to New Jersey to await the result of the biopsy. When it came, it confirmed our worst fears. Liz had a highly malignant form of cancer, but a type from which, if it is caught early enough and properly treated with radiation and surgery, the patient has an eighty-five-percent chance to recover. Our next step was to enroll her in the best cancer-care program we could find, and she chose one with an excellent reputation, at a nearby medical center.

After a month of daily radiation treatments followed by a month's rest, she underwent a radical and devastatingly serious operation. Until the time of the surgery, we had all had high hopes for a completely successful removal of the tumor and a quick and permanent recovery; but while she was still in the recovery room, I talked to a member of the team of surgeons who had operated on Liz. She told me bluntly that they had found the cancer already spread far too widely for any hope of being able to remove it completely by surgery, and that Liz had no better than a twenty-percent chance of long-term survival, even with further radiation and chemotherapy treatments. That was indeed a body blow to my hopes for my dearly beloved child, who had faced the approaching ordeal with such good spirits and courage. I found it hard to say, "Thy will be done" and mean it.

The next six months proved to be a growing nightmare, made bearable only by the support of my Higher Power, the AA program and my friends in it, and the magnificent example of Liz's courage and cheerfulness in the face of growing adversity. From the day of the operation, she was never completely free of pain, nor did she get one single break in her battle against the steady spread of the dreadful disease.

Liz wanted me to take care of her—she had no one else to turn to. Her mother had been living abroad for the past nine years, while Liz and I had shared the stages of my battle for sobriety and her teenage rebellion and dropping-out from school, through to growing maturity for both of us. Single-handed, she had made up her schoolwork and gotten into college, achieving a sophomore record of As and Bs. Between us, we had found an increasing realization of mutual love and respect.

With the wonderful cooperation of my wife, who could not leave New Orleans, I temporarily pulled up my new roots in my adopted city and moved back to New Jersey, where I had spent so many years drinking and had finally gotten sober. My home group there welcomed me back with true AA love and compassion and was to be a constant source of support for me in my coming ordeal. At one of their meetings, a young speaker from another town said that nothing really bad had happened to him in his life, until his father had died recently of cancer. He said he had gained a great deal of humility from the experience.

I began to realize that until now nothing really bad had happened to me, and that my only hope of surviving the tragic event, which was inevitably coming, was again to borrow heavily on whatever credit I had in AA. I realized that there are times when we can give something back to AA in service, and other times when we must again take from AA, even after many years of sobriety. I began to know how much I needed AA and how little AA needed me, and to be humbly thankful that a loving God brought me to our Fellowship, for indeed, it represented my only hope.

There is no happy ending to this story. Liz's health steadily deteriorated, and she died only about ten months after the cancer was discovered. But she died magnificently, cheerful and uncomplaining to the last. The memory of her courage through all her suffering and the knowledge of my desperate dependence on AA and my Higher Power when things were almost more than I could bear will, I hope, always keep me humble and grateful.

J. V. B.
New Orleans, Louisiana

Fire in the Holler OCTOBER 1987

So often we hear things in meetings that help us though we don't even realize it until much later. A very dramatic example of this happened to me recently.

The first weekend in May I drove to Lexington, Kentucky, from my former home in Millstone, a little town in the Appalachian mountains, to attend some meetings. It's about a three-and-a-half hour drive, so I spent Saturday night there with a friend in the program.

Sunday morning I went to a speaker's meeting. The speaker told a very moving story. He said when he'd had about eighteen months of sobriety he'd come home from a meeting one night to discover that his house had burned down, and all four of his children had tragically been killed in the fire. His message was simple—he said it was God as he understood God that kept him sober through that terrible time. He said he'd learned that nothing was forever, and that nothing, absolutely nothing, was so bad it could be used as an excuse to drink. He talked about the fire for quite some time, and even remarked on that fact, saying, "I don't usually talk about this so long but for some reason today I feel moved to share it."

I spent a few more hours in Lexington, eating lunch, shopping. I bought a box of baseball cards to add to my collection. Then I drove home.

We call the spaces between the mountains "hollers" here in Kentucky. Often you can't see the end of a holler from the start of it. I lived eight miles out of town, 300 yards up a holler. I saw the haze and smoke from the moment I made the turn, but it wasn't until the last corner, about thirty yards from the house, that I could really see what was wrong.

The house was gone, just flat gone. There was a pile of ashes two feet deep, a few cinder blocks, and nothing else. All I had left was a shirt, a dirty pair of socks, a few boxes of books stored at a friend's house in Minnesota, and the baseball cards I'd bought in Lexington. I'd lived too far from town to be able to get insurance, so there'd be no chance to recoup anything financially. I don't know how long I sat there sideways in the driver's seat of my pickup, my feet dangling and my mouth hanging open, thinking, It's gone, everything is just gone ...

When I found someone in town who could tell me what had happened I learned the house had burned late the night before. It had already been a smoking ruin when I sat in that meeting Sunday morning and heard that man say, "Nothing, absolutely nothing is bad enough to drink over."

In the Big Book it says sometimes we, alone, have no defense against that first drink. I know that day I didn't—in fact the first person I found, unaware that I'm an alcoholic, offered me a beer ("You need a drink," she said).

But I kept thinking about that man. I kept thinking, If he could stay sober, I can too, and that is what got me through until I could reach my own friends in AA.

I don't even know his name. I had no reason to make a point of remembering it at the time I heard it. I think he was from Cincinnati, but I'm not really sure. In a way it's not important—we don't have to know each other to help each other. I will always be grateful for his experience, strength, and hope, for it became my own.

L. O.
Minneapolis, Minnesota

How the Universe Works

NOVEMBER 2006

(Excerpt)

At two years [sober], I thought getting married would help me to feel better about myself. That only lasted fifty-two days. She ended up in a psychiatric ward and I sat on my couch with a loaded gun. But I didn't drink.

At four years, I was let go from the company I had been at for twenty-two years. I didn't drink.

At six years, my alcoholic girlfriend refused to move out of my house and got a restraining order. I moved out. She died of cancer two years later and I didn't drink.

At eight years, I opened a recovery bookstore and thought I could save the world. I lost everything within three years. But I did get to read a lot of books—and I didn't drink.

I have been fired from a very good job, laid off from another, taken a job at a lesser salary—and I didn't drink.

You see, between God and AA I can get through any situation as long as I don't pick up that first drink.

I have spent the past twenty years changing the way I think about myself. I am a student of life just trying to learn how the universe works. The most powerful lesson I have learned is that it all happens inside me. My perception of any situation is in my control—I have a choice about which way my mind will react. I try my best to look for positive solutions; I take my problems to my sponsor or I let my friends at a meeting know what is going on inside me.

One day at a time, with God's guidance, I plan to never drink again. I must always remember, however, that "the monkey may be off my back, but the circus has not left town"—and it never will for this alcoholic.

JOHN L.
Pinellas Park, Florida

A Horse Named Zachary

FEBRUARY 2004

In sobriety, I have witnessed many miracles. The miracle I wish to describe here is somewhat unusual. It involves a horse. The horse arrived in my life when I had been sober eight years. A series of difficulties, some of which arose from life on life's terms, and others which were, as the "Twelve and Twelve" puts it, "calamities of [my] own making," had left me scalloping along a deep emotional bottom.

The events which brought me to this bottom were a series of losses. I had returned to school in sobriety. I worked full time and attended night classes. Two months before I graduated, my beloved grandmother died after a long, painful illness. My amends to her was to give her care during her final days. There was no time to grieve because I was busy studying, working, trying to get a job.

One year later, my father died. My sobriety had disturbed him greatly. He had lost a drinking partner. Worse still was the fact that when the fog cleared, I realized how damaged our relationship was, and could not tolerate it. For years, I had coped with this discomfort by drinking it away. Without a chemical buffer, I withdrew from my father. My retreat angered and saddened him. He had a massive coronary during chemotherapy for lung cancer. I was unable to make amends to him before he died.

During the ensuing year, I took in a sixteen-year-old foster child, who shared my home for seven months before leaving to drink and drug. I had hoped to carry the message to her, but she did not want anything I had.

That same year, I fell in love with a married man. I thought the relationship was the fulfillment of all my hopes and dreams. I was wrong. He left his wife, then changed his mind. In the process, he revealed himself as someone other than the person I thought I loved. This loss left me stuporous with despair. Then my great aunt Lucy, the last of my East Coast relatives, died in August 1998.

By September, I had succumbed to the violent twists of my emotions. I awoke each day contemplating suicide. The ache of anguish in my chest was unremitting. I went to meetings. I talked to my sober friends and my sponsor. I worked a Fourth and Fifth Step pertaining to my love affair, and began in earnest some long-neglected work on Steps Six and Seven.

Nothing helped. I remained trapped in my overwrought emotional landscape. I didn't want to drink, but dying seemed increasingly like a reasonable solution to my problems. The feelings nearly felled me in their intensity. Luckily, God, as I have come to understand him, knew all about me. He sent a messenger.

The horse belonged to a sober friend. We became friends partly as a result of our common interest in horses. I had ridden since childhood, with long hiatuses caused by drinking, injuries, and insufficient funds, but had never lost my love of these fine animals.

My friend needed help with the horse. She asked if I would like to ride him one or two days a week to help keep him fit. Since I had little to do besides working and going to meetings, I agreed.

The horse's name is Zachary. He is an Appaloosa gelding with a meteoric sprinkle of brown spots on his white hindquarters. He is as exquisitely sensitive as any alcoholic. Because of his coloring, he did not fit in with the bays and chestnuts of the horse show world. He was challenging to ride, as he insisted on having things his way. He forgave my blunders grudgingly but gently. He was moody, personable, loving, and undecipherable. We were much alike.

Having to ride Zachary gave me a reason to show up someplace. It was not unlike having a coffee commitment, but the horse could not be deflected by excuses. He demanded my attention. If I failed to appear to work him, he suffered. I could not ignore this. Gradually, I began to forge a relationship with him. During the couple of hours I had with him each week, I forgot how bad I felt. In Zachary's presence, I was often able to cry about the people I missed, something I couldn't do in meetings. Zachary was nonjudgmental and deeply sympathetic. He never offered unwanted advice.

The horse and I began to work together. We had a good trainer, who contributed knowledge and practical suggestions. Then we were ready to compete. We entered a combined training event in October 1999. I have had many types of highs in my life—performing as a professional musician, taking a near-lethal combination of drugs and alcohol, falling in love—but the exhilaration of this event, with its combination of dressage, which is disciplined movement on the flat, arena show jumping, which demands courage and discernment, and the astonishing rush of cross country jumping, was better than anything I'd done yet. I had formed a true partnership.

I had also formed a partnership with another human being. The friend who invited me to ride shared her life and her horse with me. We had a common bond—the well-being of a sentient creature who was dependent on us. Our friendship, always refreshing, deepened measurably. As a result of our horse companionship, I found myself with a surrogate family.

Riding in the event began my escape from the emotional prison I had constructed. That might be the only miracle I have to describe; and it is sufficient in and of itself; but the story continues. Zachary pulled a suspensory ligament after the event, and went through a long rehabilitation. He was never really sound enough to compete again after that. But I kept riding. I had discovered a quality which I never suspected I had: loyalty, even in the face of disappointment. When I was drinking, and even in sobriety, if my expectations weren't met, I left. I had suffered all of my life from a fear of abandonment, a terror that kicked my drinking into high gear. Eventually, to avoid being left, I became the abandoner. I did not abandon my horse. Even when all I could do was walk him around the arena on a lead line, his presence restored my serenity.

Instead of a competitor, Zachary became the Ambassador of Goodwill. He is much beloved at our barn for his personality and humor. He has mellowed, too. But more importantly, Zachary helped me carry the message of AA.

I invited my pigeons and anyone who expressed an interest, to meet my horse. On the hour's ride to the barn, some of them opened up to me in a way that they had never previously felt able to do.

A woman I know in the program who had a tempestuous sobriety came to the barn one day. She loved racehorses and learned to handicap, but she had never ridden. She took her first ride on Zachary. It made a change in her. She still talks about this experience.

Another friend from AA adopted a son. This boy was deeply disturbed, the victim of unspeakable abuses. He, too, took his first ride on my horse. While he was in the saddle, he listened and took direction, because Zachary taught him it was important. He had to be in touch with his body, something that was nearly impossible for him, because balance on a horse is imperative.

Zachary carries the message that there is fun to be had in sobriety. He has posed for silly pictures, and eaten half a ton of peppermints extended to him on trembling hands. He has won the trust of the newly sober. He has graciously permitted himself to be ridden by inept and unhappy people. He has served as a Higher Power, a conversation piece, and a talented teacher.

I have no doubt that Zachary's appearance at a time when I

needed him most was the work of God. He deepened my faith. I had always suspected that God's attitude toward me was one of barely tolerant exasperation, if he cared at all. Zachary, the Ambassador of Goodwill, gave proof of the miracle of God's love.

AMY G.
West Hartford, Connecticut

The Care of God DECEMBER 1999
(Excerpt)

Faith in a power greater than myself is something that I'm very grateful for today. But that wasn't true in my early sobriety.

For the first five years of my sobriety, I couldn't grasp the idea that something else was in control of my life. I really thought that I was in control. Just ask the people who were around me. I was the director that the Big Book refers to. I was really good at telling people what to do and how to do it. I had no idea how to just "let go and let God." Even though I tried to control every aspect of my life, the first few years in recovery went pretty well. My job was going well, I met and married my husband, and we started a family. Life was good.

Then my life started to crumble around me. I had quit my job to stay home with our son and to help my husband with our business. Within a month of being home, we found out we were going to have another baby. We were very excited. About a month later I realized something was wrong with the baby. To make a long story short, I lost the baby, hemorrhaged and almost died, and found out I had a rare form of cancer caused by an abnormal pregnancy. I was devastated. I found myself at the Mayo Clinic in Rochester, Minnesota, not believing this was happening to me. I was going to have to go to the Mayo every week for chemotherapy—indefinitely. If that weren't bad enough, my mother died of a rare form of cancer two weeks after I started my treatments. I was lost. Why was God doing this to me? I thought he was supposed to be a loving, forgiving God. Even though I was surrounded by doctors, nurses, and the hundreds of people who walk in and out of the Mayo every day, I found myself alone, frustrated, and angry.

I remember sitting in the hospital bed getting ready for my first treatment. I was looking at my Big Book thinking, I need a meeting. I looked in the phone book, called the hotline number, and found a group that met every day at noon just three blocks from the Mayo. I went that day. What a relief—I wasn't alone anymore.

I threw myself into AA. I had always averaged three meetings a week, and now I wanted to go to as many as I could. I wasn't sure why. I wasn't afraid I was going to drink, because the compulsion to drink had been lifted from me after my first meeting. But I needed meetings. Something was telling me to go.

I was very honest with the staff at the hospital about my alcoholism and my desire to go to that noon meeting every day that I was there. With an IV in my arm, I was allowed to go, provided I was strong enough to be out of the hospital.

Between my home group meetings in St. Cloud and the Downtown Group meetings in Rochester, I stayed sober and learned a lot about myself. I found that I was emotionally and physically stronger than I ever thought. I found out what true friendship is and what unconditional love is. But the biggest thing I learned was that I don't control a damn thing. Everything that was happening to me was out of my control. In order to stay somewhat sane, I had to learn how to "let go and let God" and turn things over to the care of God as I understood him.

LIZ B.
St. Cloud, Minnesota

Relief Pitcher FEBRUARY 2007

For years, I only saw meaningless pain and suffering, both in my own life and in the lives of those around me. It baffled me. My own fundamental dishonesty kept me from seeing that most of my suffering was self-imposed or brought about by my own actions. Once I saw this—by working the first five Steps of the AA program—the suffering in my life gained some meaning.

At a recent AA meeting, we read about Step Seven in *Twelve Steps and Twelve Traditions* and I was reminded that pain could be a teacher.

Only when I accept both the pain and the joy in my life do I build my character into what my Higher Power wishes it to be. Either God is everything, or God is nothing. My choice—everything or nothing—determines whether I experience life with humility or humiliation.

In baseball, the manager brings a relief pitcher into the game when the starting pitcher gets in trouble. Sometimes, it takes a while for me to recognize that I've shuffled God into "relief pitcher" status and tried to control my life, once again, with my own power and will. If I forget that God keeps me sober, I inevitably slip back into believing that I can manage my life, change my character, and exert power over others.

I am blessed to be an alcoholic who has found a connection with a Higher Power. The Promises say, "No matter how far down the scale we have gone, we will see how our experience can benefit others." If I live my life with the intention of serving God and my fellows, nothing is without purpose. It can all be useful. When I remember this, I am blessed and grateful in that moment. Sometimes, I need reminding from my Higher Power or from the voices, faces, and arms of AA.

NICK H.
Oak Park, Illinois

My Best Day Sober DECEMBER 2000

My name is Brian, and I am an alcoholic. In my area of Texas, we usually give the date on which our continuous sobriety began. This, of course, is optional, but I seldom have heard anyone share their strength, hope, and experience in AA who did not at some time during the course of the conversation make reference to how long they have been sober. I have not had a drink of alcohol since January 1, 1964. I was thirty-eight, middle-aged and young, at the time, and now I am middle-aged and older.

I tell you this to explain that I have had over 13,000 days of continuous sobriety in AA, and life in general has been good. In retrospect, some of my best days sober might not have been the happiest days, and some of my saddest days were not my worst days sober. In fact, some of my better days in sobriety may have been those days when I knew that a drink would have temporarily reduced the pain, but I did not drink.

It was a very sad day when my wife received word that she had been diagnosed with "the big C." But I did not consider taking a drink, so it was a very good day. It was a very happy day when the doctor announced that surgery had corrected the problem completely. I did not need to drink to celebrate, so it was a very good day. It was a very sad day when our baby son was diagnosed as having a seemingly unacceptable birth defect. I did not need a drink, so it was a very good day. It was a very happy day when the doctor announced that the problem had been completely corrected. I did not need a drink to celebrate, so it was a very good day.

It was a very unhappy day when I realized that circumstances beyond my control had made continuing my employment of thirty years unacceptable. As the result of my having acquired, through the practice of the principles of the AA program, the courage to resign from the position with dignity, rather than become bitter, it was a good day.

I have had the God-given privilege of walking through many dark valleys with friends who could not or would not accept this simple program of sobriety, but I stayed sober, so these were good days for me. I have shared the joy of walking on many mountaintops as I watched seemingly hopeless alcoholics obtain and maintain continuous sobriety. These were good days. There have been deaths of relatives and friends through suicide and murder, accidents and illness. But I stayed sober, so these were not all bad days for me either.

My brother's son did not like war, but he willingly went to Vietnam. He was eighteen. During the very first hour of his very first day of action, he was killed. This was not a good day, but before joining AA, I might have become bitter. So in a sense, this was not as bad a day as it could have been, for me.

There have been too many thousands of days and too many seemingly miraculous events in my sober AA life for me to single out one day as the best. So in keeping with one of the last things our beloved co-founder Dr. Bob told his friend and co-founder Bill W., I have adopted the philosophy of "Keep it simple." Therefore, since today marks not only the last day of my life to this date, but also the first day of the rest of my life, and since I have come to believe that the best is yet to come, I think today has been my best day sober.

BRIAN G.
Lubbock, Texas

THE TWELVE STEPS

1. We admitted we were powerless over alcohol—that our lives had become unmanageable.
2. Came to believe that a Power greater than ourselves could restore us to sanity.
3. Made a decision to turn our will and our lives over to the care of God *as we understood Him.*
4. Made a searching and fearless moral inventory of ourselves.
5. Admitted to God, to ourselves, and to another human being the exact nature of our wrongs.
6. Were entirely ready to have God remove all these defects of character.
7. Humbly asked Him to remove our shortcomings.
8. Made a list of all persons we had harmed, and became willing to make amends to them all.
9. Made direct amends to such people wherever possible, except when to do so would injure them or others.
10. Continued to take personal inventory and when we were wrong promptly admitted it.
11. Sought through prayer and meditation to improve our conscious contact with God *as we understood Him,* praying only for knowledge of His will for us and the power to carry that out.
12. Having had a spiritual awakening as the result of these steps, we tried to carry this message to alcoholics, and to practice these principles in all our affairs.

THE TWELVE TRADITIONS

1. Our common welfare should come first; personal recovery depends upon A.A. unity.
2. For our group purpose there is but one ultimate authority—a loving God as He may express Himself in our group conscience. Our leaders are but trusted servants; they do not govern.
3. The only requirement for A.A. membership is a desire to stop drinking.
4. Each group should be autonomous except in matters affecting other groups or A.A. as a whole.
5. Each group has but one primary purpose—to carry its message to the alcoholic who still suffers.
6. An A.A. group ought never endorse, finance or lend the A.A. name to any related facility or outside enterprise, lest problems of money, property and prestige divert us from our primary purpose.
7. Every A.A. group ought to be fully self-supporting, declining outside contributions.
8. Alcoholics Anonymous should remain forever nonprofessional, but our service centers may employ special workers.
9. A.A., as such, ought never be organized; but we may create service boards or committees directly responsible to those they serve.
10. Alcoholics Anonymous has no opinion on outside issues; hence the A.A. name ought never be drawn into public controversy.
11. Our public relations policy is based on attraction rather than promotion; we need always maintain personal anonymity at the level of press, radio and films.
12. Anonymity is the spiritual foundation of all our traditions, ever reminding us to place principles before personalities.

Alcoholics Anonymous

AA's program of recovery is fully set forth in its basic text, *Alcoholics Anonymous* (commonly known as the Big Book), now in its Fourth Edition, as well as in *Twelve Steps and Twelve Traditions, Living Sober*, and other books. Information on AA can also be found on AA's website at www.AA.ORG, or by writing to:

Alcoholics Anonymous
Box 459
Grand Central Station
New York, NY 10163

For local resources, check your local telephone directory under "Alcoholics Anonymous." Four pamphlets, "This is A.A.," "Is A.A. For You?," "44 Questions," and "A Newcomer Asks" are also available from AA.

AA Grapevine

AA Grapevine is AA's international monthly journal, published continuously since its first issue in June 1944. The AA pamphlet on AA Grapevine describes its scope and purpose this way: "As an integral part of Alcoholics Anonymous for more than sixty years, Grapevine publishes articles that reflect the full diversity of experience and thought found within the AA Fellowship. No one viewpoint or philosophy dominates its pages, and in determining content, the editorial staff relies on the principles of the Twelve Traditions." AA Grapevine also publishes La Viña, AA's Spanish-language print magazine, which serves the Hispanic AA community.

In addition to magazines, AA Grapevine, Inc. also produces books, eBooks, audiobooks, and other items. It also offers a Grapevine Online subscription, which includes: five new stories weekly, AudioGrapevine (the audio version of the magazine), Grapevine Story Archive (the entire collection of Grapevine articles), and the current issue of Grapevine and La Viña in HTML format. For more information on AA Grapevine, or to subscribe to any of these, please visit the magazine's website at www.AAGRAPEVINE.ORG or write to:

AA Grapevine, Inc.
475 Riverside Drive
New York, NY 10115